SHINE YOUR
LIGHT

SHINE
YOUR LIGHT

Illuminating Stories to Inspire
Resilience, Self-Discovery,
and Positive Change

POSITIVITY LADY
PRESS

SHINE YOUR LIGHT

Illuminating Stories to Inspire Resilience, Self-Discovery, and Positive Change

A LIGHTbeamers Book by April Adams Pertuis
featuring these contributing authors:
(in alphabetical order)

Debi Choi

Blythe Cox

JoAnne Dykhuizen

Cami Foerster

Marcia Murff Tabor

Jill Ore

Sandra Pantoja

Jennifer Pivnick

Belinda Sandor

Rikki (Cindy) Shaw

Evelina Solís

Amey Stark-Foust

Library of Congress Control Number: 2023915167
ISBN: 978-7327858-5-4

Positivity Lady Press
Robbinston, ME 04671
www.positivityladypress.com

This anthology is a work of creative non-fiction. All of the events depicted are true to the best of the author's memory. Some names and identifying features have been changed to protect the identity of certain parties. The author in no way represents the views of any company, corporation, or brand. Views expressed are solely those of each author.

This book is dedicated to the thirty-four women who came together to share their stories in our collaborative books. "Shine Your Light" completes the trilogy of books in the LIGHTbeamers She Gets Published series.
Our stories are made possible by the
women who have gone before us.

Table of Contents

INTRODUCTION

INTRODUCTION

With each new collaborative book we begin, I expectantly wonder what sort of stories the Spirit will conjure up in these women. What bold moves will they make by sharing pieces of their story?

Will each woman challenge herself to go deep into the waters of her story in such a fashion that allows her to see it in a new light? And will that story be one others can digest and use for their own illumination?

Without a doubt, that's what the authors of this book have done. They have gone into the deep, dark abyss of their stories and brought back treasures of inspiration, encouragement, teachings, and wisdom.

As a story coach, I get excited anytime a woman comes to the table ready to share her story. I'm excited about what will unfold for her. I see the potential her story holds and explode with anticipation of how that woman will be transformed by her commitment to swim into the deep layers that lie inside.

I liken it to a caterpillar who transforms and grows wings. Storytelling wings.

The women authors of *Shine Your Light* have earned their wings. They have done the arduous work of extricating their stories from their own deep wells. They have drowned out the doubt, uncertainty, fear, shame, and many other emotions to resurface ashore with what can only be described as *light*. They've examined the bits and pieces of their stories that are worth your time to read. The pieces that are important to share. The bits that will fit into your own story and have you wondering where their stories end and yours begins.

Each one of these stories is so relatable and real. In many cases, utterly raw. Both heartbreaking and beautiful at the same time. Because that's what stories are—the perfect alchemy of darkness and light. The light swallows up the darkness much more when the stories are shared with other people. That's why this book is titled *Shine Your Light*.

We hope that our stories will connect you to something in your own deep ocean—that you will discover something you need to keep swimming through life and that will inspire you to take positive action. May the light shine for you in a way that feels warm and illuminating.

Feel free to hop around the chapters in this book and settle in with a writer as if she were sitting across from you at a cozy coffee shop, telling you her story. And if her story moves you in any way, find her contact information in the bio that immediately follows her chapter and reach out to her.

Why? Because knowing our stories do indeed make a difference will shine a light back to us.

You, our dear reader, are a huge part of this process. We wrote these stories with you in mind. So thank you, thank you, thank you for being here.

May these stories shine the light you need today.

We are forever grateful to have you with us.

xo,
April

Chapter 1

FACE THE DARKNESS

April Adams Pertuis

"Suffering is not part of our punishment in life—it's part of our awakening."

I could feel the tightness in my chest, the shortness of breath in my diaphragm, and the sinking pit in my stomach.

Anxiety had returned.

The thoughts running through my mind were oh-so-familiar. They'd taken up residence in my head before. . . but it had been a while. I thought I was past all of that. I thought I had healed the wounds that caused me such panic. I thought having all the tools and resources in my tool kit meant I wouldn't have to deal with this dark, dangerous feeling ever again.

After all, I'd gone years without feeling anxiety to this degree. Sure, it would come and go for a day or two, but I could easily put to use all the tools and resources I had added to my mental tool kit over the years to knock it out of the way:

Journaling.

Meditation.

Prayer.

Long walks in nature.

Talk therapy with my husband.

Positive affirmations.

Don't get me wrong—the books, practices, habits, and tools work most of the time. After all, they'd been working for me for more than thirteen years. . . . But anxiety is sneaky; it tricks you into thinking it's gone away, when in truth it's maniacally concocting new and skillful ways to overcome you when you least expect it.

Anxiety doesn't make sense when you're battling it. All the books you've read, the mindfulness practices you've implemented, and healthy habits you've adopted seem to go out the window in a nanosecond when anxiety is able to find a sliver of an opening and step in to gain its footing.

The familiarity upon anxiety's return was haunting. All of a sudden, I realized I was right back in that same "closet of darkness" I had been in nearly thirteen years earlier when a financial stressor had triggered me into a tailspin.

And here I was again . . . in the tailspin.

The first time anxiety took up residence in my life was shortly after the birth of my second child. I had two kids under the age of three. I had put my career on temporary hold for motherhood. My husband, Kyle, was a partner in a business that was thriving, and we were living in a dream house with a mountain view. By all accounts, we were checking off all the boxes and enjoying the semblance of all-American "success."

Although I was thoroughly enjoying the newness of motherhood and witnessing firsthand the daily changes and developments in my children as they discovered new foods, learned to walk, babbled over new toys, and splashed hysterically in bubble baths . . . the reality was that motherhood was also overwhelming and exhausting. I spent most of my days wondering if I was doing it right, often finding myself at the end of a frayed rope. It looked nothing like the motherhood those perfectly polished bloggers presented online. I loved my children and wanted to be there for every moment of their lives, but I also missed my career. I missed using my brain in ways that were challenging and creative. Taking care of babies and doing the "mom thing" left me feeling like I was giving up half of myself so I could have the other half in return. I was doing what I thought was best, but in the moment, it felt like a giant piece of "me" was missing.

Meanwhile, my husband's business partnership was in the tank. The relationship had turned very toxic, and Kyle was miserable. He wanted out, but we relied on his income. He was the only breadwinner in the family, and his company paid us very well. I didn't realize how frustrated he was with his business partners (or maybe I overlooked it for the sake of my own comfort) and missed a lot of cues that he was reaching the end of his own frayed rope until one day, he came home and said, "I've told them I'm taking the week off—and when I go back, I'm going to let them know if I plan to stay."

A week? What in the world can you get together as a plan B in the span of a week? If you leave, what will we do for income? How will we pay our bills? Can't you just stay and tough it out? We have a family to think about.

That was my internal reaction to his announcement. Outwardly, I put on a brave face and encouraged him, even though panic was beginning to set in. Little did I know, this was the opening for anxiety. I was triggered around the fear of impending financial struggle and an unknown future, which would later force me to come unglued. I had no idea it was happening, but I was becoming a ticking time bomb.

At the end of that week, my husband exited his ten-year business partnership and stepped into a broiling legal battle in an attempt to dissolve the partnership equitably. He took six months off to figure out his next move, which meant we had to dip into our life savings to float us in the interim. He later accepted a consulting gig that sent him traveling on airplanes five days a week—leaving home on Sunday nights and not returning until Friday. The consulting work brought money back in, at least, but it took him away, leaving me to manage the household, which included two very young children, all by myself.

The final straw was when we opened a letter from the IRS to discover we were being audited.

The audit turned into a bloodbath. I attended most of the meetings with our accountant by myself because Kyle was away during the week. The CPA would report the findings from our IRS agent, and I'd go home with more items to worry about and pile them on top of the heap of fear that had been building for months. I'd wait until Friday to share the updates with my husband, because discussing the details of two years' worth of taxes was just too much for our nightly check-ins over the phone. Instead, I'd spend the week alone, pacing the floor and worrying about the future.

With so many big changes in such a short amount of time—the birth of a baby, the exit from a business partnership, the legal battle, the IRS audit, a new job, changes to our family dynamic with my husband traveling through the week—it all came crashing down on me one night after I'd put the kids to bed.

My usual pattern was to get the kids down and peel away to my bedroom to catch my breath after the day's thoughts had accumulated in my head. Thoughts of "what-ifs" and "we-should-haves" stormed me every night.

I would often call my mother, who was more than a thousand miles away in a different state, and talk to her as a way of calming my nerves. She always had soothing and reassuring words to help me work through my anxious thoughts, and most of the time, I would hang up the phone and feel calm enough to get myself to sleep. (God bless my mother!)

But on this particular night, my mother threw me a curveball. After listening quietly while I droned on about how hard it was to be at home alone with the kids, how we were struggling financially, how worried I was that we weren't going to be able to recoup any money from the business partnership because of the legal battle, how awful it was to have my husband gone during the week, and how terribly alone I felt . . . my mom tossed out a life preserver.

"April, why don't you just come back home to Texas. Come back here where your family is and let us help you get back on your feet. Let us help you with the kids while you go out and look for a job and get back to work. It would be good for you to have your family around you right now."

She was right. I could think of nothing more wonderful than running home to Mama. I could picture it in my head: she'd take the kids to the park or zoo and treat them to ice cream every day while I got my career back on track. Kyle could keep his consulting job, but with my extra income, we could get back on our feet and jump-start our financial growth by having two incomes again.

It sounded really good; I told her I'd think about it.

After our call, anxiety enveloped me stronger than ever before. Every ounce of "hope" and "good ideas" my mother and I had just discussed was stamped out like a candle-snuffer extinguishes the light.

Sobbing hysterically, I shut myself in my closet as I often did when I didn't want anyone to hear me crying. Afraid I might wake the kids, I sat in the middle of my closet floor, feeling the darkness that was all around me physically and emotionally. Darkness is all I remember.

When I was empty of all my tears, I looked up toward the top of my closet and saw my suitcase on a shelf. I stared at it for a few minutes while my mother's invitation replayed in my head. I stared at it a little longer, contemplating her words. I thought, *It's a pretty damn good offer.* It made a lot of sense to go back home to Texas and get support. In fact, why wait? I could just pack that bag right now . . . and get the kids packed, too. We could hop in the car within an hour and be on our way to Texas. I could call Kyle in the morning to explain that I had left everything we owned behind, and ask him to reroute his flight on Friday to Dallas instead. All of this . . . this entire life we'd built . . . we could just walk away from it and start over again in Texas.

Nothing made sense, and yet, at the same time, *everything* made sense. All logic and reason had left the minute anxiety started talking.

Rational ideas like "Make a plan to move back to Texas" turned into irrational plans like "Screw the plan, let's move tonight!"

But sometimes an irrational plan is what you need. Making plans—no matter how irrational they are—has a way of pushing anxiety back into the corner.

Slowly, I stepped out of my closet in a blank stupor. I stumbled into bed and crawled over to my side, leaving my husband's side of the bed empty. I grabbed a couple of books that were sitting on my nightstand. I had purchased them but never opened their pages.

I laid them both in my lap. I opened one and began reading. The book was written by a pastor's wife, and within the first five pages I discovered a section she wrote on "Worry" in which she shared her own battles with anxiety. She too had a hard time clinging to the present and instead fretted over all the things that might happen or could happen in the future.

I kept reading, and with each new word of her story, I saw myself. Like her, I knew my worry and anxiety was completely irrational; however, the more I read, the more I learned it was rooted in junk from my past.

Memories of my childhood surfaced. I remembered answering the phone to debt collectors when I was around ten or eleven years old. I recalled my parents' divorce and how we had to move out of the only house I'd ever known. I thought about my senior year of high school when I had received acceptance letters to several prestigious universities that I was smart enough to get into, but the tuition was too steep and my parents told me they couldn't afford to send me. I ended up taking a gap year and spent that time working two jobs to save enough money to go to the small state school down the road and pay for it all on my own.

All of these fragments came together like a mosaic, illustrating a story I'd adopted and had been carrying around with me unknowingly. A story that I'd been telling myself subconsciously for months as my husband and I navigated our own rocky financial territory: *My parents had struggled and made mistakes with money when I was growing up; therefore, I was destined to follow in their footsteps with my own mistakes.*

It started to make sense why I had been off the rails for the past several months. The stakes were so much higher now that I had a marriage, kids, and a mortgage. The minute my husband had come home from work and told me he was making a big change, I had begun telling myself that we would undoubtedly go down the same path as my parents. We would amass insurmountable debt, we'd lose our house, we'd fall apart and get divorced, our kids would suffer from the ripple effects, and their lives would be severely impacted.

This made-up story had been playing on a subconscious loop in my head for months, and I'd had no idea. Absolutely no awareness of it whatsoever. All I knew was how it made me feel: scared, worried, debilitated, and alone.

I could see how some of my false narrative had been fueled by real-time events in our life:

We would struggle to pay our bills, so debt collectors would come after us. This story was perpetuated when the IRS audit began.

We would struggle financially to the point of ruining our marriage. This story was perpetuated when my husband began traveling five days a week and our trust in each other was tested.

We'd never be able to send our kids to college. This story was perpetuated during the months when money was lean.

Each new reality we experienced perpetuated the false realities in my head.

My tailspin had little to do with our reality and everything to do with trauma I'd experienced as a child and young adult. Anxiety had taken up residence not because there was anything *real* to worry about, but because I'd been unconsciously worrying for years that I'd make similar mistakes. Worry becomes your reality when you don't have proper awareness of it.

That had been thirteen years earlier.

Since then, I'd taken personal and professional growth very seriously. I'd worked with coaches, read countless books, enrolled in live seminars and online courses. I'd spent time digging deep to see this story for what it really was—my parents' story, not mine. And to be fair, it wasn't even my parents' *real* story; it was *my version of it* formed from my lived experience and perspective. It was tainted and not all true. It was like a terrible game of telephone, where the story starts out one way but becomes distorted and discombobulated as it is retold and passed from person to person.

Over the years, I had become much more aware of my anxiety and seen the truth that hid behind it. When the pit in my belly showed up, I deployed the many tools and resources I had added to my tool kit to quickly work through my emotions.

I acknowledged the crappy money story I'd been hauling around for decades and made conscious efforts to address it at every station along the way.

So this most recent bout of anxiety had me perplexed. Why in the world was this reentering my life?

By now, my kids were teenagers. My husband and I *had* eventually moved back to Texas, but not because we needed our parents to take care of us. In fact, it was quite the opposite: they needed us to take care of them. Specifically my dad. His health had declined significantly, and he was no longer able to work. He needed more hands-on care, and we'd moved back home a few years earlier to help him manage. Three years later, Dad had passed away from cancer. Now, three years after his passing, this "closet of darkness" feeling had returned.

I had been going through some big changes personally as I navigated the onset of menopause. We had just bought an older home that needed a ton of renovations. And our oldest son was beginning his college visits in preparation for his senior year of high school. Kyle and I had built our own businesses and were running them from our home offices. Things were humming along, yet for months I'd been feeling pings of anxiety that were becoming more and more frequent.

Except this time, I was so busy managing the hum of life—kids, business, clients, social commitments—that I ignored the warning signs and didn't pull out my anxiety tool kit to manage the pings. I got lazy and let my guard down, paving a clear entry point for anxiety to return. It didn't even have to sneak in—I left the front door wide open.

The only way I know how to describe it is that it felt like I was living in a house of cards that could come crumbling down at any moment. Anxiety had arrived with a menacing message: "You are just one step away from losing it all. You better watch out."

That wasn't reality, but remember, anxiety doesn't live in reality. It plays on the fear of the future. The what-ifs and you-should-haves.

Our deepest fears usually come from the place that needs our highest attention—wounds that need to be tended to even when we believe we've healed them. As with a scab, it doesn't take much more than a nick to reveal fresh meat and blood just below the crusty surface.

A scratch of a fingernail is all it takes.

That brings me to the day anxiety reentered my life, uncovering new layers of that old wound. Throwing myself into deep prayer in an attempt to understand this new version of anxiety, I was pointed back to something I had overlooked the first go-round:

Getting help.

I had never once given counseling or therapy a thought when I battled it out with anxiety more than thirteen years earlier, or during the many other mini-battles I'd experienced over the years. But this time around, it became the obvious choice.

Well, sort of obvious! It took a few dips into the darkness and a few solo attempts of knocking anxiety back outside the gate before I realized this new version of anxiety was smarter and stronger than the last guy.

And in a really prophetic way . . . a way in which only the Holy One can provide . . . I was sent to help an organization that had once helped my dad.

When Dad first got sick, we immediately called in hospice care per his oncologist's recommendation. For nine months, the hospice nurses, case workers, chaplains, and volunteers helped us navigate the incredibly choppy waters of terminal care. They made everything easier. I cannot imagine what it would have been like to navigate Dad's care and ultimately his final days without them.

It had been three years since his death, and an opportunity showed up for me to volunteer my time and talents to help the hospice organization raise money at their annual gala. I immediately said yes.

In talking with the hospice staff, I learned more about the grief counseling they offer family members after a loved one transitions.

I knew about these services because after Dad passed away, grief counselors reached out to me personally. At the time, I declined their offer, assuring them I was okay. But when they shared with me some of the stories of how grief counseling was serving and helping so many families in our area—in a variety of ways—I began to see a light I hadn't seen before.

Grief is a weird and unusual visitor. It's very hard to see grief because, like its friend anxiety, it tends to sneak into your life through a back door. It isn't always dressed the same and comes wearing many disguises. Working on the fundraising project, I got to hear many stories from other people of what their grief journey looked like, how grief showed up, and how counseling was helping them.

Grief didn't look like I thought it would. In my mind, grief was the result of the loss of a loved one, and came immediately after the loss. I thought grief would look like sadness. But for me, it was showing up in ways that made it difficult to define it as grief. Grief triggered a lot of memories I held around personal losses—not just the loss of a loved one, but loss of a dream, loss of an idea, loss of a path I looked forward to exploring. And the grief brought anxiety back to the surface for me. The bottomless pit feeling in my stomach that I couldn't make go away.

Anxiety is a grief by-product.

Upon deeper reflection, I could feel God saying to me, *April, you've asked me for direction on how to fight this anxiety and remove it from your life. I'm trying to show you how. . . . Pay attention!*

Counseling was a tool I'd never added to my tool kit.

Counseling or therapy had never, ever crossed my mind. I always thought I was "strong" mentally and didn't need that sort of help. I prided myself on doing the deep work and touted all the books and courses and coaches and prayers and journaling as my medicine.

But now, the idea of it seemed so obvious. Why hadn't I considered it before?

Sometimes the obvious isn't that obvious when you aren't looking for it. And sometimes the obvious is hidden and you have to be intentional about hunting it down.

I believe this most recent visit from anxiety was more of a gift than it was a nuisance. It was a wake-up call.

Trauma can live like an undercurrent in your life without ever sending shock waves to alert you it's still there. It's easy to live with trauma and adopt it as a "this is just how it is" way of life.

For years, I batted anxiety away and accepted that I was one of those people who dealt with the annoyance. I added more tools to my tool kit and kept going. I became more self-aware and proactive. I was adept at dealing with the "this is just how it is" version of my life with anxiety as that undercurrent.

And the truth of the matter is, it helped me grow and evolve. I was no longer that scared, young mom who felt dependent on others for her own security (financial and otherwise!). I was no longer afraid of taking risks and making bold financial moves. I could easily start a new business, make big investments, and make plans for the future because I felt secure around money for the first time in my life.

My "money story" got smaller and smaller over the years—so much so, I was almost convinced that I had healed it completely.

But I hadn't.

The undercurrent was still there.

As I looked deeper at this most recent version of anxiety, I began to trace it back to grief. Death and loss can be transposed into other areas of your life that mimic similar experiences.

The normal dose of grief I felt around the loss of my dad was transposed into a larger-than-life version of grief around the loss of many things: the loss of my childhood home, the loss of an ideal family with two parents who loved each other and lived happily ever after, the loss of a dream education, the loss of security, and so much more.

This idea of grief has helped me see how I was covering up my pain by letting anxiety rule my thoughts about the future.

I don't believe my money story will ever go away because it's connected so deeply to real, lived experiences I've walked through. These are experiences that don't get erased; they are imprinted on our souls and encoded into our emotions.

But I do believe I can rewrite that story and create a much better ending for myself.

I don't believe our suffering is part of our punishment in life—it's part of our awakening. With each anxiety-induced bender I went on, I learned something new.

At first, I gained critical awareness. Later, I learned how to incorporate important tools and resources. This last round has taught me how to ask for help and concede that I don't have all the answers.

Those three steps are pretty important in all areas of personal and professional growth, wouldn't you say?

Raise your awareness.

Add tools and resources.

Ask for help.

The stories we've been given are about personal discovery. Anxiety has been a good teacher for me in this way. I've learned how to self-regulate on my best days, and how to acquiesce and lean into others on my worst days. But one thing I know for sure is that I am not alone.

Grief is a newer teacher, and I will spend some time now in counseling discovering its ways. For the first time, I can talk about anxiety without feeling afraid of it. I'm actually quite intrigued to learn more about it, because the more you travel a road, the more you familiarize yourself with its curves. Going deeper to understand how both grief and anxiety work will help me navigate the path ahead.

It's a new journey yet a familiar one, and I'm eager to get on my way.

APRIL ADAMS PERTUIS

April Adams Pertuis has been a storyteller since she was a little girl, hiding out in her room writing secret poems and scribbling stories on the wood slats underneath her bed. An extreme sense of curiosity led her to ask a lot of questions when talking to people, wondering what secret story was hiding inside. It's no surprise that keen interest led her to journalism school and a lengthy career as a television journalist, video producer, and brand storyteller.

In 2014, frustration over the stories being shared on social media led her on a quest to go deeper with her work. Desiring to make an impact on women's stories, she created LIGHTbeamers. Today, April leads the LIGHTbeamers Community, full of women who are curious about their own story, and she helps them excavate the layers of their story through various online courses and coaching programs. She also hosts the highly-rated Inside Story Podcast, and is the co-creator of the LIGHTbeamers Author Program and Storytelling Symposium, all of which give women a platform to share their stories with the world.

When April isn't dreaming up ways to equip and empower women through storytelling, she is hanging out with her husband and two kids, traveling somewhere in the mountains, or soaking up the good Texas sunshine and eating tacos.

Chapter 2

EXTEND YOURSELF GRACE

Jennifer Pivnick

"Learning how
to stay in a place
of peace while
trusting God is a
powerful tool."

I live life with an abundance mindset. I believe there is a gift or an opportunity everywhere and in every situation. I am a recovering perfectionist who has learned how to make simple changes that helped change my negative and self-limiting beliefs. Now I live life with a peace that surpasses all understanding based on a foundation of faith that cannot be broken.

I wasn't always this way. . . . On the outside my life seemed perfect, or at least I tried hard to make it look that way. I was often asked how I did it all. On the inside, I felt like I was stuck in quicksand, and I was sinking fast. I needed to break free from the cycle of negative thinking and self-doubt. The still, small voice in the back of my head said, *You are worth more than this. There is more to life than how you are living it.* But I translated it as *Work harder, do more, be better.* I believed in God. I knew Jesus. I said I trusted him, but did I really? As I have learned, believing in Jesus and trusting him are two very different things.

Trust in the Lord with all your heart and lean not on your own understanding; in all your ways submit to him, and he will make your paths straight.

Proverbs 3:5-6 (New International Version)

I needed a different life. I carried the weight of the world on my shoulders, and the balls I had been juggling for years were starting to crash down around me. My husband always had the potential to be a great man, but he could not let go of his many addictions. I was eighteen when we met. In the beginning he seemed like the answer to all my problems. He was nine years older than me, successful, smart, and driven—a positive change from the heroin addict I called Dad. Now, twenty years later, he was just another problem I needed to fix. I was exhausted, sad, and, honestly, pretty angry that I had repeated a toxic family cycle.

I hated that I was financially dependent on him to maintain the lifestyle we lived with our four teenage children. I worked hard to help support the household, but my income didn't match his. Luckily, I found a passion for marketing and events at the sports club where my daughters played. Unfortunately, anytime I found success, he somehow managed to sabotage it, from embarrassing me at an event to disappearing for days. That put me in crazy mode to do whatever I could to keep my life from falling apart at his hands. For some reason I held on to the belief that I could fix him if I loved him enough. Then I would have a happy life just like everyone else.

When I look back now, I can see why I stayed stuck for so long. My life had always been full of chaos. If I wasn't in the middle of crazy, I knew it was coming. I seemed to be a magnet for dysfunction. I expected bad things to happen. I trained my mind to look for the worst, because I thought that would prepare me to handle it. I was determined to fight the good fight by fixing everything and everyone around me. I could easily see the right thing everyone else should do, but for myself it was clear as mud. The negative tapes that played in my head constantly reminded me that I was not worth much. I needed to learn how to control my mind and not accept every thought as truth.

My life was a mess. Could I really walk away from a twenty-year marriage? It felt like such a selfish choice. I didn't want to hurt my children; I wanted to protect them from pain. But the example of marriage they had in front of them was full of manipulation, lies, and dysfunction. The only way I could make this choice without feeling overwhelmingly guilty was to give it to God, to lay it at Jesus's feet—this giant mess of a life that was mine and mine alone.

I opened my closet and pulled out my old prayer journals and thumbed through the pages of brokenness, worry, stress, and fear. I realized that I had been in this place for a very long time. And in that moment, I finally understood that it was not my job to fix my husband or anyone else. I needed to figure out how to let go of what was breaking me.

I had to learn how to trust God in every area of my life, not just when it was an emergency or I was in pain. I wanted what he wanted for my life. But to get there I had to look in the mirror and own my part of the story. I realized I alone had the power to choose the life I wanted. I was not a victim of my circumstances; I was there because I allowed myself to be there. I had participated in the breakdown of my marriage. I had taken the easy road or looked the other way many times because I didn't want to deal with what life would look like otherwise. To be honest, I had been doing the same thing in my relationship with Jesus for a long time as well.

I started to intentionally focus on the good in my life and not the bad. Every day I wrote down three things I was grateful for. That small change helped me look for blessings in my life. I started expecting good things to happen to me. *God is for me, not against me,* I would remind myself. I saw first-hand how powerful that shift in perspective was. Gratitude changed my focus. It not only turned what I had into enough but enabled me to start seeing opportunity everywhere.

The final straw did come, and it broke the camel's back. The ugliness of divorce ensued, and the pain it caused my children was real. It sucked. But the decision was made. There was no stopping this forward motion. Maybe God would fix my husband, maybe he wouldn't. But it was officially no longer my problem to solve. I would pray for him and do my best to wish him well. I felt free but also very scared. I could feel Jesus by my side, and somehow, that was enough.

During those difficult days, I fought hard to keep the negative tape in my head at bay. I filled the house with worship music so that the devil couldn't get in. But at night it was a different story. I was able to fall asleep easily from exhaustion, but the 3:00 a.m. wake-up call from my brain was no joke. The never-ending list of worries and fears would run through my head. *Fine*, I would think. *I will acknowledge these fears and play the "what-if" game one time and that's it. "What if I can't pay this bill or buy the kids what they need?"* . . . *"It will be fine; I will find another way."* I would answer each negative thought with a positive outcome. Then I would turn on a church podcast. If you have ever fallen asleep in church, you know it's the best sleep. Turns out, it works the same in the middle of the night with a church podcast on.

> For I can do all things through Christ,
> who gives me strength.

> Philippians 4:13 (New Living Translation)

I usually liked to keep myself busy taking on everyone else's problems so that I didn't have time to deal with my own. But I was tired of doing that. It just left me feeling overwhelmed and unappreciated, which in turn made me resentful and reactive. Learning how to stay in a place of peace while trusting God is a powerful tool that I was determined to master. It required me to move and grow in totally different directions, and opened my eyes to a new thought process I hadn't known existed.

Honestly, it's embarrassing to admit this. But I used to have zero understanding when other people did not agree with me or think the way I thought. I just didn't get it—there had to be something wrong with them. When I truly understood how other people managed their emotions and processed information, it allowed me to not only give them a break but give myself one as well.

That is why developing my emotional intelligence was an important step on this journey. I dove headfirst into studying all the different types of personalities. It was so interesting to understand what motivated others. That knowledge gave me insight into the massive differences and similarities among people. It was fascinating to see how other people managed their emotions and interpreted the world around them. It really helped me learn that not everything is about me and to not take everything so personally, which was a surprising step toward a life of peace.

It also solidified my belief that we are all here to learn and grow. Not one of us is better than anyone else. We are all on the same path, but we're at different stops along the way. Some of us have more baggage than others. A few have learned how to let go of what no longer serves them and some haven't, and that is perfectly okay. Their path is theirs and mine is mine.

Therefore, there is now no condemnation for those who are in Christ Jesus, because through Christ Jesus the law of the Spirit who gives life has set you free from the law of sin and death.

Romans 8:1-2 (New International Version)

I focused my efforts on improving myself instead of trying to fix everyone else, starting with the password on my computer. I changed it to *Worth More*! It reminded me daily that my value was not defined by other people. Every time I opened my computer, I had to physically type in the words *Worth More*! It was annoying at first, but slowly it started to transform my thoughts about myself.

I've learned that growth is not always done in a straight line—sometimes it is two steps forward, three steps back. I was working hard to fight through negative thoughts. I still felt like I had to earn everything. Grace was not something I could easily accept. I knew I needed to trust that God was in control and that his timing is perfect. But I wasn't sure how to do that on a consistent basis. It was very difficult to wrap my brain around letting God work things out for me.

I am an action person; waiting is not my strength. I reminded myself of Martha in the Bible story when she complains to Jesus about Mary not helping. His response to her is that Mary is doing the right thing—not Martha. That story always bugged me, because I felt like Jesus should have magically made everything be done so Martha could sit down too. It has taken me years to figure out that the lesson he was trying to teach is to seek him first, and then he will work everything out—not the other way around.

Fortunately, Jesus showed up when I asked him to. He stayed. He listened. He responded. He repeatedly made himself known to me. I would pray specific prayers and he would answer them, although not always in my timing and not always in the way I liked. Several times, he actually made me laugh out loud. He is pretty funny if you listen to him. He met all my needs and more. Bringing me the perfect job at the exact right time, and an adorable house that I could fix up and call my own. Giving me the ability to support my children in every way they needed without relying on anyone else. Honestly, the old me would have focused on the hardships of each of those blessings and not the actual miracles that they were.

The road was rocky and challenging, but I remained strong and full of hope. The days I intentionally turned my focus to Jesus, instead of trying to do everything myself, I felt unstoppable—which replaced the feeling that nothing I did was good enough. I intentionally focused on his truth. I would write in my prayer journal verses that helped me, like "He makes me lie down in green pastures," and "I can do all things through Christ, who gives me strength." This changed my default setting from negative thoughts that brought death to positive ones that breathed new life into my soul.

As a divorced single mom, I made sure to take the time I needed to heal and establish new ways of thinking. My focus remained on my children, but I also had big dreams; I just didn't know what they were yet. I had never really taken the time to sit down and clarify what I wanted to achieve in this life. I believe that God gives us the desires of our heart so when we follow our dreams, we find the life we are meant to have, because God is the one who places the seed of those dreams in our hearts to begin with. We just need to take the time to figure out what they are.

I started by asking myself, *If I could have any life I wanted—any life—what would it be?* I had never allowed myself to think about that, because I was too busy doing the next thing on my never-ending list of to-dos. It was time for me to dream big. Funny enough, I felt guilty even trying to sit and do that. *What a waste of time*, I automatically thought. I recognized how easy it was to fall back into the trap of limiting self-beliefs that were trying to hold me back. I finally understood that what I thought about and focused on would be the largest indicator of success for every area of my life. Learning how to dream big was a challenge. I had to do it with intention; I couldn't expect everything to just fall into my lap. I still believe in hard work.

I needed to do more than just think about it. I sat down with a blank sheet of paper and broke my life into different categories: work, home, kids, love, friends, health, faith. If I could have any life I wanted—anything—what would it look like? What would my days consist of, and how would I spend my time? No filter, just write it out for each category. Nothing was off-limits. If part of my dream was to sit on the beach eating bonbons, then so be it. I wrote down things I knew I wasn't qualified to do, never previously thought possible. Now I can clearly see that life moves us in the direction of our dreams. If we have no goals or dreams, then we simply move in the direction of fulfilling other people's goals and dreams.

I didn't expect to experience such clear life-changing successes in every area of my life so quickly. It has been crazy to see some big dreams and some little dreams come to light right in front of my eyes. I am now the president of an insurance company that specializes in youth sports, with a growing nationwide footprint. I have met a wonderful man who loves me and my children. I expect good things to happen to me, and I am open to what God wants for my life. I now understand why Jesus says that when you pray, you must believe that you have already received it. It is not only the foundation of faith but the secret to living in peace that surpasses understanding.

I still get off track from time to time, but I recognize that life is about learning from our mistakes. We don't just arrive at perfection one day. That is a weird lie that we all somehow seem to believe. Knowing that Jesus loves me more than I will ever love myself has helped me learn to accept myself for where I am currently, not where I think I should be. I love that I am passionate and creative. I love to make the world around me beautiful and a better place to be. I certainly do not have all the answers, but I know my worth. I no longer tolerate being around anyone who makes me feel less than. I own who I am, but I still work toward being who God made me to be. I choose to speak life, not death, over those I love and even those I don't. I live intentionally both personally and professionally, with both goals and dreams solidly in their place.

This chapter is meant to shine a light on the path I walked down and share the hard-earned knowledge that Jesus is the only way to peace. Not everyone will decide that changing their whole life is the answer for them, but when you turn to God, he will make your path straight. He will either fix the situation you are in or give you the strength to handle it while he works in the background to provide another way. But first you must choose to trust him.

In this life we are meant to grow. Change is inevitable; it is the one thing we are guaranteed. Stay aware of the traps that try to pull you back into old mindsets and habits. Every choice you make, good or bad, matters. So, with prayer and petition, take it to God and choose to believe the best outcome for every given situation.

And watch him eagerly show up and do the same for you that he has done for me.

> If we are sure He hears us when we ask, we can be sure He will give us what we ask for.
>
> 1 John 5:15 (New Life Version)

ABOUT THE AUTHOR
JENNIFER PIVNICK

Jennifer Pivnick shines a light on what is possible when you break free from the chains of a negative mindset. As the mother of four children in a challenging marriage, she spent all of her energy trying to fix others, leaving little for herself.

Now, as a self-proclaimed recovering perfectionist, she has learned how to dream big and trust God. She puts that wisdom to work as a speaker, author, and business owner dedicated to improving the world around her. She outlines the steps that can help you leave behind what is holding you back from living a life of peace, passion, and purpose.

You can learn more or contact her on Facebook @jenniferpivnick or Instagram @jennifer.pivnick

Chapter 3

CHOOSE TO LOVE

Blythe Cox

"The journey and the destination are worth it."

Y'all, I've battled a thick southern accent my whole life, so when people meet me for the first time, they usually ask me where I'm from. I'm from the armpit of Texas, also known as the Golden Triangle, which is in the southeast part of the state. It's a hot and humid place, home to lots of mosquitos, swampy bayou gators, crawfish boils, Janis Joplin, crude oil, and the murder of my family.

To some it's like a paradise, but to me it's more like the curse of the Bermuda Triangle. Once you're there, it's hard to get out. Now, don't get me wrong, it'll always be home. But it's not where my heart is—it's just where it was broken into a million pieces.

I have to say my story is hard to tell, and it sure as hell has been hard to live through. With that said, though, whose isn't? My story is filled with love, heartache, drugs, sex, and rock and roll. Throw in some Jesus, sweet tea, and a whole lot of crazy, and voilà, that about sums it up. So, buckle up, buttercup, this small-town Texas girl's about to take you for a ride.

It was the most beautiful day in June 2006, and I felt fantastic. It was strange, though: my entire life, I'd never felt the way I did that day. Peaceful, content, and truly happy. I remember saying out loud how great a day it was. It was definitely the calm before the storm. The weeks before had been a bit chaotic, but all in all somewhat normal in my world. My father and stepmom had decided to separate and were going through a very difficult time. He was convinced she was seeing someone else, and she was convinced he'd lost his mind, so she had decided to leave.

That night I woke up at 12:36 a.m. with a very strong urge to call my dad. I mean like wide-eyed, fully awake. I sat on the side of the bed and picked up the phone, recalling his cell number. I held the phone and thought, *This is crazy. He's fine, Blythe, you're being weird.* So I put the phone down and soon fell back to sleep.

The following day my daughter and I were supposed to go on a playdate with some friends: McDonald's for lunch and a trip to the park, the perfect summer day in the life of a four-year-old. That morning, I woke up, walked into the living room, and turned on the TV for my daughter. It just so happened that the news was on. I made my way to the kitchen to make a cup of coffee. I could vaguely hear the news anchor describing the violent details of a triple murder/suicide.

My heart dropped. My hands instantly went cold and clammy, causing my coffee cup to fall from my hand and shatter on the tile floor. I tried to remember how to breathe while cautiously realigning my gaze with the TV. I stood there staring at it, hoping that what I was seeing wasn't true even while I knew it was. In the breaking news story, no names were given, and no pictures of people were shown. The newsman described the scene of what appeared to be a domestic violence situation gone to its most horrific extreme. A local woman and her children had been murdered, a police officer had been shot, and the husband had committed suicide in the home.

As the news anchor continued to speak, they cut to a video clip of the side of the house. All I can remember seeing is the distinct 1970s-style brick. I couldn't hear anything else. There was no denying what had just occurred. My life crumbled in front of my eyes.

Still, I had hope. My hands and body shaking, I picked myself up. Stumbling to the phone and sick to my stomach, I struggled to dial my grandfather's number. The rings seemed to last forever as time slowly slipped by. He gruffly answered, "Hello!"

"Pop, where's Dad?"

"He's dead," he said angrily. I hung up and dropped the phone while running to the back door to get outside. I fell to my knees on the ground, burying my face in the grass. I then lifted my heavy body to the clouds, screaming at the top of my lungs, "WHY GOD, WHY?"

At that moment I realized my husband was at work. Sobbing uncontrollably, I called his job. Barely able to speak, much less be understood, I said, "Is Chris there?"

The young man who answered knew it was me, and said, "Ma'am, he's on his way home."

My next thought was *My mother, where's my mother?* "No, God," I said. "Please, not my mother too."

Trembling inside, I called her. My stepfather answered and spoke in a voice I'd never heard before. "Blythe, we're on our way to you. Your oldest brother is alive. Your sister's at the lake, but we're trying to get her on the phone. I love you. Here's your mother." At that moment, I felt a sigh of relief and guilt. My mother was alive. This could've happened to us!

No one was there with me but my precious little girl, who by now was screaming and crying, scared and trembling. Her words finally caught my attention as she begged me to reply. "Mama, what did Grumpy do?" she yelled. At that moment I realized my innocent child's heart was breaking right in front of me. My daughter was only three years younger than my baby sister, who had just been brutally murdered by our father. The guilt and shame choked me. How could I protect her?

I got down on my knees, held her tear-stained, red, sweaty little face in my hands, and said, "Sweetie, Grumpy just broke my heart."

I stood in the bathroom silently staring into the mirror, unable to recognize myself. They say the eyes are the windows to the soul. It's true. My eyes were so blue at that moment, and so empty. I was weak and afraid, feeling like my heart was literally being torn and ripped apart, dying inside my body. Staring deeply into my soul I said the words "It is finished." It wasn't until years later that I would come to know and understand the meaning of those exact words, the final words of Jesus Christ as he died on the cross.

Let me give you a little backstory.

I grew up in a relatively small town, with small-town views, a church on every corner, and lots of town gossip that somehow made its way to the dinner table. People thought the Internet was fast, but I beg to differ. The women of a small town are much faster. My grandmother used to say, "You can't sling a cat around your head without hitting a church in this town." It's so true! She also had a saying that "you can't beat out of the bone what's born in the blood." That's the one that always got to me. As a kid I wasn't sure exactly what it meant, but as an adult, unfortunately, I found out.

My parents met in 1973, married in 1975, and divorced in 1989. That was a long time for them to be married to each other, trust me. Growing up in the eighties, my childhood was interesting, to say the least. My mother was in a band, my dad was an ironworker, and they fought most of the time. The constant fear of the next fight loomed around me. Their heated arguments usually turned ugly and violent. Thank God we had my grandma Balla—she was our saving grace. Had it not been for her, there were times we wouldn't have made it.

Not long ago I counted and realized that by the time I was ten years old, I'd moved twelve times. That's a lot of uncertainty. My parents separated in 1987, not long after my sister Blair was born. Their relationship boiled down to a lack of trust. There were some good times, but the bad ones outweighed the good for sure, or at least it did in my eyes. My father was a very handsome and charismatic man. His smile lit up a room, but he was also a liar and a cheat, couldn't keep a job, and had had a very messed-up childhood.

Compared with my two sisters, my parents' divorce hit me the hardest, and by that I mean emotionally. My mother had a nervous breakdown, so I helped her take care of the everyday things. I helped her pay bills, grocery shop, cook, and clean, all while helping take care of my little sister Blair. I did my best to keep the peace so my parents would stop fighting. I protected my sister and tried to make life as normal as possible. Although it was far from normal, I did the best I could at nine years old to make it feel that way. Hearing your mother cry herself to sleep every night and seeing her broken takes a toll on you. It took a toll on my grades, my social skills—everything, really. All the while, I just wanted to be like all the other kids.

After my parents' divorce, my dad and stepmom had two boys and a little girl. It's sad how I wasn't able to have a real relationship with them. I was twelve when my oldest brother was born and nineteen when my youngest sister was born. I tried to be there and form a relationship with them, but I was much older and labeled the "other woman's" daughter. I wasn't given the chance. As time went on, my father slipped back into his old ways and once again found himself in a relationship that was out of control. They tried to make it work, but with each new baby, their relationship got progressively worse. I believe my stepmother realized he wasn't all she'd dreamed of. Now, don't get me wrong, she wasn't very kind to my sister Blair and me. She tolerated us, but we weren't hers, nor did she treat us like we were.

Their relationship also became volatile and violent. That's when she decided to leave. She filed a restraining order against my father and was in the process of filing for a divorce. It was only weeks later that he brutally murdered her, my youngest brother, and my youngest sister, and killed himself, but not before injuring a police officer. By the grace of God, my then thirteen-year-old brother was able to escape his wrath and survived. He's now thirty, happily married with two precious children and doing very well, all thanks to God.

There's a thin line between love and hate. I mean, how do you move forward from something like this? I can tell you—you don't. Not unless you have a good support system and know Jesus. But get ready, because you're going to have to fight some battles along the way. Satan has tried to destroy my life. I'd already fought some battles and had some pretty crazy stuff happen in my life. I mean, this wasn't the first time someone in my family had been murdered. My dad's father, my grandfather, killed my grandmother. When I was thirteen, I was sexually assaulted. I wound up in emergency surgery, fighting for my life. Two years later, at the age of fifteen, I had a miscarriage. I pretended like I was fine, kept it a secret, and tried to move on. It wasn't until I was in my thirties that I faced the reality of having lost a child.

The nightmare of events and the aftermath of my father's actions debilitated me. I literally could not eat or sleep, and my body was in constant pain. The sound of sirens gripped me with fear. For years I was unable to hear screams or guns going off without panicking. Not only did my mental state take a major dive but so did my marriage. I was physically sick all the time, was afraid of being alone, and suffered in a state of grief. To top it all off, I was appointed as the executrix of my father's estate. Add in a slew of extended family who hate you and a whirlwind of money issues, and you've got the perfect storm.

I managed to muster up the courage to live each day. It was a daily battle that took courage and strength that only God could provide. I prayed constantly for God to take the pain away from me. However, he didn't do so right away. I was haunted by my father's past, and questioning my life.

About two years later I finally found relief from the pain and gripping fear that had overwhelmed me my entire life. Praise be to the Lord! I asked God to give me joy, and he did.

Not only did he take away my fears and give me the gift of hope, but he promised to never leave me nor forsake me. He took me to heaven to experience something that no one in a million years could ever fathom. It was early one morning in 2008 when I woke up to my new baby, Kelly, fussing in her baby bed. I walked to her room and picked her up from the crib, and then decided to lie back down in my bed with her by my side. We soon got comfortable and fell asleep, and I was instantly in heaven.

It's the most beautiful place. Nowhere on earth is more beautiful. Nowhere! And the colors, wow! There's no color on earth like there is in heaven. Just imagine standing inside a diamond mixed with a pearl: that's still not as gorgeous as heaven. All you want to do in heaven is praise God. That's literally all you desire. And the light and the color, it's so gorgeous. It's like a warm, cozy blanket that engulfs every part of your existence. The light is inside you, above you, and below you, and it surrounds you with love, peace, and truth. The light is God. I didn't get to see all of heaven, but what I did see is very hard to describe because the words we use to describe anything on earth will never do it justice and do not exist here. Just believe me, you want to go!

God is real, and he loves you. Honestly, if it weren't for God, my mother, grandmother, husband, and sisters, I would be dead or off the deep end right now. Fear is real too. The Bible mentions fear approximately 365 times. That's one time for every day of the year. It is said in 2 Timothy 1:7, "For God did not give us a spirit of fear, but of power, and of love and of a sound mind" (Young's Literal Translation). That is a promise from God that I cherish.

There's a story in the Bible that during Passover, Jesus rode on the back of a white donkey toward the gates of Jerusalem as the crowd welcomed him and sang praises, shouting "Hosanna!," which means "save now" in Hebrew. It was quite a happy moment, but as Jesus got closer to the gates, he stopped and cried. Why did he stop and cry? I believe his heart was broken. Maybe he was even anxious. He knew his fate, yet he loved the people. In the Garden of Gethsemane, Jesus prayed three times to God, asking him, "My Father, if it is possible, may this cup be taken from me. Yet not as I will, but as you will" (Matthew 26:39, New International Version). Jesus knew why he had been chosen, but that doesn't mean he was excited about it. Nor did he want to have to endure a painful death. But he chose to.

Today's world is filled with massive amounts of stress, fear, and anxiety, and it doesn't seem to be getting any less stressful or any more certain. It's becoming increasingly difficult to navigate the ups and downs of life. I can promise you, I did not want to have to endure the pain I've experienced in my life either, and I gave up many times along the way. But God picked me up out of the darkness of my pain long enough to remind me that I am a child of the King.

I had to make a decision to forgive. I had to make a decision to receive love. I had to make a decision to be grateful. I had to make a decision to have joy and peace. I had to have faith and trust God that there was a purpose for my pain and suffering. I had to decide to accept myself, my faults, and my past, and realize that those things did not define me. I decided to bury the lies I was believing and move forward instead. I decided to love, and that included loving myself. Hurt people hurt people. And if I'd chosen to be consumed by the darkness hovering over my life, I could easily have taken another path down the road to destruction.

Instead I chose to rise above, be the person God called me to be, and make a difference—by helping others who are hurting, sharing my story, giving back to my community, and ultimately doing my best to be a light amidst the darkness. It's a choice. It's not going to be an easy road to travel, but the journey and destination are worth it. My journey brought me to a new town, with new faces, new opportunities, and the chance to make new memories in a beautiful place with the ones I love. I'm not certain what's around the corner, but I know that whatever it is, God will open the door and see me through to whatever lies ahead. But first I have to decide to trust him to get me to the other side.

When I was a child, I had a little stuffed white unicorn with a beautiful yellow-gold horn. I'm sure some of you had a stuffed animal or a toy you lugged around as a child too. This unicorn was very special. She had no name, just Unicorn. I carried her everywhere. She was dragged around, stained with dirt and tears, and just frankly worn smack out. Her mane was all matted up, so we washed her, but then her tail and her hooves started to tear. I carried her around anyway, loved her anyway, even when she looked like a wreck and probably should've been thrown away. I kept on sewing her back up. I loved my unicorn so much, nothing could replace her. I cherished her, and she meant something to me.

To someone else—really anyone else—she probably looked like an ugly old stuffed animal. But to me, she was beautiful. She'd been there for me when no one else was, to soak up my tears, calm my fears, give me hope, and share my dreams. Her stitches were the signs of a life well lived. They gave her character and showed that she could withstand the toughest days. She was always there for me, carrying me through some of my darkest and brightest days. Had I not cared for, loved, and cherished her, she would have remained tattered and torn. But she was treasured, more precious to me than anything in the world.

I believe I'm like the unicorn in this story. Although I'm tattered and torn, I am precious in the sight of God. I am cherished and adored. I am unique and beautiful with all of my life's scars and imperfections. I am loved and worthy and more than a conqueror. I have been healed and comforted, brought out of the darkness, and sewn back up to be made whole again.

Maybe that's you too. No matter how hard life gets, remember, we were chosen for a time such as this, to fulfill a unique purpose. You don't have to do it alone. However, you do have to make a choice to move forward. Trust that God will be the light to your path. Deuteronomy 31:6 (NIV) says, "Be strong and courageous, Do not be afraid or terrified because of them, for the Lord your God goes with you; he will never leave you nor forsake you."

ABOUT THE AUTHOR

BLYTHE
COX

Blythe Cox is a former Texas beauty queen whose life has been far from perfect. Her story is riveted with brokenness and tragedy yet conquered by love and hope. At the age of 26 her life took a major turn with nowhere to hide the past. She had a choice to make to either live life with purpose or to give up and allow life's circumstances to steal her future. It was during these storms that she discovered peace and the true meaning of love. Having foraged through a lifetime of grief and pain, Blythe's made it her mission to help others see that there's a light at the end of this tunnel we call life.

Blythe has spent over twenty years in the financial industry and is an active member of many local organizations that focus on community development, business leadership, education, service, and helping women and children in need. She's married to her high school sweetheart Chris and together they have two beautiful girls, Kylie, and Kelly. She lives in the beautiful Texas Hill Country where she enjoys spending time with family and friends, summer days floating the river, and listening to live local music.

Chapter 4

HOLD ONTO YOUR PURPOSE

Evelina Solís

"God isn't done
with you yet."

Growing up, I was a force of boundless energy, health, and vitality. Sports, extracurricular activities, church, and serving my community were my passions, defining my existence. But on a spring night in 2006, destiny chose to test me as I stood before a sea of expectant faces, hosting an awards presentation for university students.

I found myself gasping for breath, ensnared in the clutches of a pulmonary embolism. In the hospital room, each breath was a testament to my weakened lung, every movement an agonizing pain. But it was the arrival of my parents from Texas, along with a contingent of extended family members, their anxious faces etched with concern, that truly awakened me to the gravity of my health predicament.

Days blended into a haze of suffering until, against all odds, I emerged from the hospital in a wheelchair, attached to an oxygen tank—a fragile resemblance of my former self. My mom and dad, unwavering pillars of love and support, became my constant companions. In addition, a devoted home health nurse aided my journey toward recovery, and their combined efforts kindled the flame of hope within me.

As the months passed, my loved ones and a diligent team of physicians reached a consensus: my healing would come with lots of prayer and the warm embrace of my parents and extended family within the comforting confines of Texas. It was there that I would find the love, support, and daily assistance necessary to forge a path back to wholeness.

The next three years brought persistent bruises, low-grade fevers, swelling, joint pain, headaches, and overwhelming fatigue. An army of doctors stood bewildered, unable to decipher the cause of my symptoms, leaving me adrift in a sea of uncertainty.

Although my case remained a mystery, I was making positive strides in my health journey and working at the University of Texas at Austin as well as running my own speaking, coaching, and consulting company. Then, on July 28, 2009, my life changed forever. I was about to deliver a presentation to a couple of hundred teachers visiting from Spain and had just finished plugging in my USB to pull up my PowerPoint presentation on the computer. I walked to the front of the room to start my training. Suddenly I began to have a seizure.

My dad, who was there with my mom to cheer me on, ran to me as fast as he could to catch my fall. He didn't make it in time. I collapsed on the floor, convulsing. He and my mom cried out for help. I can only imagine how helpless they felt in that moment. My parents were traumatized and petrified.

My sandals flew off my feet. I bit down on my necklace, causing my jaw to lock, and broke my left front tooth. The fear-stricken teachers tried to get someone to dial 911, and then some of them ran out of the room, yelling for help. The paramedics arrived, and I was rushed by ambulance to the nearest hospital. The goal once I was stabilized was to transfer me to St. David's North—the hospital where the team of doctors who had treated me previously could work together to find answers and treatments. As soon as I settled into the ICU, I took another turn for the worse.

"Code blue! Clear the room! Run, go get the cart! Start the compressions! There is still no heartbeat. Hurry, grab the paddles! Ready! Clear! Again! Clear! Again! Clear! Okay, team, we have a heartbeat again. Great job. This young lady gave us a huge scare. She is going to have a very long road to recovery ahead of her."

Why do we have to find out we are dying to truly begin living? Waking up in a hospital bed fighting for my life gave a whole new meaning to life being precious, fragile, and fleeting.

The next thing I can recall is waking up in a hospital room strapped down and hooked up to machines. I had lost my cognitive and motor skills and didn't recognize my loved ones. The neurologist would regularly ask me questions such as "What is today's date?," "What is your name?," "Who is the president of the United States?," and "How old are you?"

Honestly, I thought I was responding with the correct answers that made sense, but I could tell by the doctor's facial expressions he didn't understand. It was super frustrating that I couldn't articulate in words the images in my mind.

I felt trapped inside my brain. Little did I know my brain was on fire. I went into days of confusion, fear, exhaustion, memory problems, emotional dysregulation, and behavioral changes. Having three seizures within the first couple of days caused me to flatline each time. I exhibited childlike behavior for weeks. A doctor would ask me every day if I knew the date and the president of the United States. I had no clue. Also, I was scared when doctors or family walked into the room, because I didn't recognize them or my surroundings. Every day, I needed assistance bathing, combing my hair, brushing my teeth, and eating and walking. The tasks we take for granted every day were my struggles.

After the three seizures, I slipped into a coma and woke up in a catatonic state. Looking back, I briefly remember the details of the presentation that traumatic day of July 28, 2009. The next day I can recall is August 12, 2009. I had been fighting for my life, slipping in and out of consciousness, for two weeks.

My fragile body was unrecognizable. I lost weight and muscle mass, lying in a hospital bed for so many days. I was hooked up to a feeding tube for nutrition, an oxygen tank to help me breathe, a catheter to drain my urine, and IVs for medication. Some of the aggressive medications like steroids had horrible side effects. The medication altered my mood. My hair fell out in chunks. I had difficulty staying asleep, and my skin was breaking out worse than when I was a teenager.

Doctors were frustrated that they couldn't figure out what was causing my body to react in this abnormal manner. The hospital ran every test they could imagine. I was poked and prodded. They pumped me full of immunosuppressive therapies and chemotherapy. Nothing seemed to be working. My weak body couldn't handle much more. After doctors' reports, it sounded and looked like there was little hope of survival, and recovery was unlikely.

Memories flooded my head. I dreamed of returning to the life I loved and once knew. I was frustrated that no one understood anything I was trying to do or say. I felt helpless that I couldn't speak, eat, walk, or move. It was miserable to not be able to communicate with the outside world. I was upset that my health continued to deteriorate. The only comfort I found was in the Lord. I went to Him with some big prayer requests for my miracle. The one thing I knew I could do was pray and fight to regain a "normal" life. I know prayer is powerful and changes things.

I was hopeful that if I was breathing, even with the help of machines, I still had a slim chance of surviving. All I needed was a glimmer of hope to continue fighting. Most days in the hospital, it was a struggle living minute to minute. Moving my fingers and toes or blinking were huge accomplishments.

I knew if I was alive, I still had purpose. If I was breathing, God wasn't done with me yet.

Some thoughts and internal conversations in my head while I was in the hospital really stuck out at me. I had this ongoing conversation with God, saying, "If you really want me to continue being a speaker, educator, coach, and journalist, then you are going to have to make a way for me to speak, eat, walk, and move again. I know you didn't bring me this far to bring me only this far. You are going to have to raise me out of this deathbed just like you did Lazarus.

"I promise to speak about your goodness and share your inspirational story to anyone who is willing to listen. I will let others know that my life is your miraculous work. I will continue to live my life as a servant leader to bring you honor and glory. I will learn from my past mistakes and be more intentional with my borrowed time. I just want the chance to hug and kiss my family once more.

"You can move mountains! Nothing is impossible for you! You have reminded me in your Word that when I am weak, you are strong, and I can do all things through Christ who gives me strength. Also, you work out all things for good for those who love you and are called according to your purpose. You didn't say *some* things you work out for good but *all* things. I need your strength, grace, and mercy now more than ever.

"You also say in your scriptures that the plans you have for me are to prosper me and not to harm me, but to give me hope and a future. I am waiting on you, Lord, to renew my strength. I will mount up with wings like eagles. I shall run and not be weary, I shall walk and not faint. I am clinging to your promises. I'd love to see what you have in store for my future. At this point, I don't know how much longer I can hold on. I'm tired. You are all I have and need. Help! Please, hear my cry, Lord.

"On the other hand, if it is not your will for me to continue my work here and you decide this is the end of my earthly chapter, then please take me now, because I am in excruciating pain. I pray that if it's time for me to go, you will comfort my family and let them know I am at peace, pain-free, and happy in heaven with you. I love them all so much!"

At the same time I was crying out my frustrations to the Lord, my family and friends were praying around the clock, interceding on my behalf. They did not allow the bad news from doctors to keep them from standing in the gap. Prayer is powerful, and it works.

Amid the desperation for answers, the rheumatologist approached my parents about administering higher doses of chemotherapy. It was the only solution the doctor could suggest. He informed them that with all the doses of medication they had already pumped into me, there was a chance my body wouldn't handle it, and I would die. They had very little time to decide. I have a praying mom and dad who refused to accept the doctors' diagnoses as God's prognosis. They leaned into their faith and cried out to God. My parents asked for God's will to be done in my life. They know that every child is a gift borrowed from God. My parents felt they didn't have any other choice at this point than to agree to the higher doses of chemotherapy. They knew that in the end the Lord is in control and has the final say.

As hard as it was going to be to accept my fate, my parents knew they had to be prepared for the outcome. They had to find comfort in His Word and peace in the crazy storm.

When my mom sat by my bedside and looked into my eyes many days, I was disconnected and distant. She no longer saw that familiar sparkle in my eyes. I'm sure it was discouraging for her as a mother. She asked God to keep me safe and in the palm of His hand. She cried out for the opportunity for us to be able to communicate with each other once more.

Moments later, with the few words I could mumble, I gave her the sign she needed. I told her that God had never left me. I had been at peace, seen His light, and felt His warm presence, and was in the palm of His hand. She was blown away, because those had been her exact thoughts and words during her prayers, which she had never spoken out loud. She knew beyond the shadow of a doubt that it was her answer from God. After that extraordinary moment, I could no longer speak. I was back to being a prisoner in my own mind. The thoughts in my mind didn't translate into words out of my mouth. It would take months of speech therapy to articulate thoughts, ideas, and feelings again.

That was the pivotal moment in the hospital when my family knew that God hadn't forgotten about us. He had never left us and was in the details of our story. The few words I spoke to my mom were confirmation to her, Dad, and my two brothers, plus the rest of the family, that I was going to live.

God wasn't done with me yet. I was breathing, so I still had a purpose. I had lives that I needed to change and inspire.

My incredible, patient, and loving parents knew that when I made it out of the hospital, I was going to have a long road to recovery. They were eager to get me home. It was going to take an entire village to get me back on my feet. Everyone was going to have to step up and help in some way. Caretaking responsibilities for someone in my situation were going to be extensive. Doctors warned my parents that I might exhibit childlike behavior forever. They were willing to do whatever it took to see me healthy, happy, and thriving again. They also knew that God was going to use me in a mighty way.

Family members came from Illinois, Indiana, Florida, and Texas to help my parents with the caretaking responsibilities in the hospital and later at home. They knew my parents and brothers were going to need their prayers, love, and support more than ever. I couldn't be more thankful to God for blessing me with a big family that comes together in times of crisis and celebration.

They were praying, advocating on my behalf, researching symptoms, asking lots of questions, and comforting us in the times we needed it the most.

My hospital routine required daily full-body wipe-downs and bed baths. My family would take turns combing my hair, brushing my teeth, teaching me to write the letters to spell my name, pushing me in my wheelchair, walking with me after my physical therapy sessions, reading me the Bible, praying with me, and playing Christian and upbeat music and inspirational sermons and speeches. They even told me funny stories to try to jog my memory. My behavior and responses remained childlike. There wasn't a quick fix to this illness.

The multiple tests and scans in the hospital led to a diagnosis. I had lupus cerebritis that eventually became systemic lupus erythematosus. It was such a relief for my family to have answers so that doctors could start treating it. Finally, they could put a name to the disease that had almost taken my life. They were ready to use their greatest weapon to fight it: prayer.

Lupus is called the cruel mystery, because it is complicated and unpredictable. It's very hard to diagnose. No two cases in the world are the same. On average, it takes six years for lupus to be diagnosed. It is often mistaken for other autoimmune diseases. It is also referred to as "the great imitator," because it mimics so many other illnesses. Lupus symptoms can also be vague, come and go without warning, and change over time. Some people have heard of this widespread disease, but they don't really know what it is.

Lupus is a beast! It can affect any organ, any tissue, or the blood at any time. It causes extreme fatigue, fevers, hair loss, headaches, joint pain, stiffness, swelling, muscle pain, skin sores, rashes, and low-grade fevers. With lupus, your body acts as if it is allergic to itself. You feel like you have the flu year-round and never feel completely rested. It also compromises your immune system, which means I get sick more easily, for longer periods of time and more often.

According to the Lupus Colorado website, lupus is more prevalent than AIDS, sickle cell anemia, muscular dystrophy, cerebral palsy, multiple sclerosis, and cystic fibrosis combined. It is estimated that 5 million people worldwide have lupus, including 1.5 million Americans, and that 16,000 people will receive a diagnosis of lupus this year. Further, according to the Lupus Foundation of America, it is believed that 10 to 15 percent of people with lupus will die prematurely from complications of the disease.

After twenty-five long days in the hospital, I no longer recognized the reflection looking back at me in the mirror. Lupus wreaked havoc on my body. I was in a wheelchair, dependent on help for everything. I was lost trying to figure out who I was and the life I had. I was trying to put together all the missing puzzle pieces. Many months of physical, occupational, and speech therapy helped me rebuild my life.

Also, the long road to recovery meant moving back in with my parents until I could get back on my feet. I never imagined that in my late twenties, my parents would have to take care of me again. I thought I would be taking care of them. It was a very humbling experience for a responsible, driven, and independent woman who had spent most of her twenties chasing dreams and crushing goals in the spotlight as a leader, speaker, educator, and radio/TV personality. My parents and grandma are the real MVPs for giving up their lives to care for me.

Lupus has been one of my greatest teachers. I may have lupus, but lupus doesn't have me. It doesn't hold the pen in my story, God does. He isn't done with me yet!

These are the greatest lessons lupus has taught me:

My problem is now my platform. My mess is my message. Every good testimony comes with a test. I am no longer a victim; I walk in victory. I am chosen and not cheated. My trial is now my triumph.

Life is precious. I must make every moment count. I am on borrowed time. I must choose what I do with my time wisely. Time is my greatest asset. I will never get it back.

Family is everything, and friends make the world brighter. I will cherish them. They will always be there for me and love me.

I have a choice to become bitter or better because of my trials. Cultivating an attitude of gratitude is powerful! Gratitude, thankfulness, and appreciation are where I find my strengths, gifts, and power.

Words are powerful. Life and death are in the power of the tongue. Words can build someone up or quickly tear them down.

I am given only one body to live in. I love it and take care of it.

I need to be kind to others. I never know what battle someone is fighting. I need to pick up the phone more often to let someone know they matter. I need to tell them I love them. In addition, I need to forgive my enemies so I can experience freedom and laugh more often.

It was during my hospitalization when I physically did not have a voice that I found my purpose and platform. It was in my weakness that I relied on God's strength to carry me through recovery. He never left me. Surprisingly, I do not see lupus as a curse but as a blessing to live full and die empty with my borrowed time. I realize that I am not the cat with nine lives.

Ever since July 2009, I have been on this mission to bring hope and change lives. I am an inspirator and a voice for the voiceless. I want people to see themselves the way God sees them, *not* how their disease, illness, hang-up, weakness, or past tries to define them. I want people to live healthy, happy, more fulfilled lives by using their God-given gifts to walk out their purpose while they still have time.

God is good! I have returned to speaking, coaching, and consulting in addition to teaching enrichment classes at a small private Christian school. God began this great work in me years ago, and He is seeing it through to completion. In 2022, I was blessed with the opportunity to become the LIGHTbeamers Community Ambassador. We help women elevate their voice, step into their brave, and shine their light by giving them the confidence, tools, and opportunities to boldly share their story on multiple platforms. This is how I know God is real, faithful, and good. His timing is perfect. His plan for my life has surpassed my wildest dreams. I'm doing all the things I love. It's been a dream come true. I'm even blessed to be contributing to this book when fourteen years ago I couldn't write or read a single letter. God is the only explanation for these blessings. He deserves all the honor, praise, and glory.

Most importantly, God blessed me with the most beautiful gift I could ever have imagined. Just fourteen years ago, I couldn't eat, talk, walk, or move, much less function as an adult. God had different plans for me. He gave me the opportunity to experience marriage and motherhood.

Although my marriage didn't weather the storms of life, motherhood was the ultimate blessing. God's promise was to prosper me and not to harm me, and to bring me hope and a future. He delivered big-time with Hope Grace, my incredible daughter, born in 2012. She is my inspiration behind waking up, crushing my goals, and becoming the best version of myself while still battling lupus. She is the greatest combination of faithfulness, happiness, intelligence, creativity, and athleticism. She is my little ninja warrior. She is an overcomer. She is going big places.

Here we are fourteen years later, and I'm happy, healthy, and thriving. We are still praying for someone to find the cure for lupus. It continues to be complicated and unpredictable. Stress, lack of sleep, and bad food choices can trigger the symptoms. I've been in and out of the hospital several times over the past decade because of blood or kidney issues or emergency surgery removing inches from my large intestine. Some days are better than others. I still take six medications daily. I've made lifestyle and nutrition changes to help keep it under control. I'm happy to report that the last three years I have stayed in remission. The lupus journey continues. . . .

I will continue to be in the fight of my life until the day the good Lord calls me home. When I come face-to-face with Jesus at the end of my life, I want to be able to say, "I have fought the good fight, I have finished the race, I have kept the faith" (2 Timothy 4:7, English Standard Version).

I'd love His response to be "Well done, good and faithful servant" (Matthew 25:21, ESV).

Lastly, Erma Bombeck said it best: "When I stand before God at the end of my life, I would hope that I would not have a single bit of talent left but could say, 'I used everything you gave me.'"

Don't let the grave be the richest place on earth. Use your gifts now. Don't give up!

If you are still breathing, you have a purpose. God isn't done with you yet.

ABOUT THE AUTHOR

EVELINA SOLÍS

Curiosity, compassion and her unwavering love for humanity led Evelina Solís to a vibrant career as a TV/Radio personality, inspirational speaker, coach, author and educator. After Lupus threatened to steal her light and take her out of this world, Evelina emerged as a powerful advocate for Lupus, PTSD and children with learning differences. Now the unstoppable CEO of Sol2Soul radiates an infectious zeal for life and her positive energy ignites a fire to those who cross her path. She inspires everyone to live full and die empty.

When Evelina isn't shaping young minds, coaching a sport or empowering adults, she is serving at church, enjoying music, sports and traveling with her daughter, Hope. Or she can be found at the next fiesta indulging delicious homemade tacos and reveling in the warm embrace of her extended family and cherished friends. Illuminate the world with her at evelinasolis.com

Chapter 5

TRUST YOUR INNER STRENGTH

Sandra Pantoja

"Each challenge serves as a stepping stone towards strength and enlightenment."

Strength grows in the moments when you think you can't go on but you keep going anyway. — Unknown

Close your eyes and imagine a time in your life when everything is going just right. You are experiencing remarkable professional growth, and your family life couldn't be better. Life feels like a dream, filled with success and contentment. But suddenly, life throws you a curveball, flipping your entire world upside down. That was the reality I faced during the summer of 2014.

"Your name is all over the Internet," my husband said urgently, his voice filled with concern. My heart dropped as the realization washed over me: those unfounded accusations made months earlier by a coworker had gone viral, and the claims of an affair between my boss and me had spread like wildfire on the Internet. I was being wrongly accused, and the unsettling notion that someone's words held the power to drastically alter the course of my life washed over me and paralyzed me.

How could this be happening? I had always been careful with my actions and words, especially in my professional life. Growing up, I had learned the importance of integrity and abiding by social norms. I pursued an education and succeeded in achieving what society deemed as success. In 2006, I embarked on my corporate journey, landing a dream job at one of the world's most prestigious media companies. It provided me with both security and status, and the future seemed incredibly promising.

I thrived in my role and had the privilege of working under a great boss. His mentorship inspired me, instilling in me confidence and a sense of professional fulfillment. Together, we formed a great team, and I quickly became his right-hand person. Through his guidance and my hard work, I rose through the ranks. However, my naivete and unshakable belief in my righteousness shielded me from other people's resentment simmering beneath the surface and the rumors swirling behind my back. I never would have imagined that people would consider my professional success a product of a romantic relationship with my boss.

By the summer of 2014, the company was facing a lawsuit by the coworker who had made false accusations against me. She had been affected by the recent round of layoffs. Her termination seemed to have fueled a deep resentment, leading her to accuse my boss of sexual harassment and dragging my name into the legal claim, alleging that he and I had had an affair. It was evident that her accusations had nothing to do with me, but because of the constant media scrutiny on my employer, the Internet caught wind of the story, and it quickly became the subject of many gossip sites. I found myself labeled as an adulteress by people who knew nothing about me, and the helplessness I felt was overpowering. The power of the Internet to spread rumors became painfully real, and I feared the damage to my reputation was going to be irreparable.

Months before the story went viral, I sat in disbelief as the human resources rep mouthed words I could hardly comprehend: "We have been conducting an investigation into a formal complaint submitted by a fellow employee regarding an inappropriate relationship between you and your boss." In the corporate world, such allegations are serious and can lead to termination. I was scared and in shock. Although I knew the accusations were not true, I felt hopeless, because in my head, people assumed I was guilty.

The investigation took a couple of weeks to complete. During that time, all my communications were reviewed, and I was given guidelines on how to behave around my boss, such as avoiding closed-door meetings and one-on-one lunches, and not entering and leaving the building together. These restrictions made me feel guilty until proven innocent. After several weeks, the results were in: not guilty. There was no evidence that any of the allegations were true because they were completely fabricated and meritless. However, the damage was done.

The days and weeks after the story broke were undoubtedly the most difficult and challenging times I've ever experienced in both my personal and professional life.

Some of my colleagues and friends distanced themselves from me, although others showed their unwavering support and encouragement. Walking into meetings and feeling everyone's eyes on me was unbearable. I spent countless hours attempting to find a solution, including writing a letter to the people in charge of the main website that had published the story, imploring them to remove it. I vividly recall moments when I had to talk myself out of quitting my job, because I believed that staying put was the only way to prove my innocence.

My relationship with my boss changed, and I felt self-conscious about all my interactions. I became more guarded with coworkers, and it took me a while to fully trust my colleagues again. The incident made me realize that not everyone in my workplace had good intentions. I had always thought of my workplace as a supportive environment, but now I realized that it wasn't. I lost my faith in the people I worked with, an isolating experience that left me feeling helpless and alone. I felt trapped in a job I no longer enjoyed. I was afraid to leave the company and find a new job, fearing that my reputation would precede me and make it difficult to secure employment elsewhere. I felt as though I carried a burden of shame that didn't belong to me, and the thought of people judging me based on what they read online was too much to bear.

To make matters worse, my husband worked for the same company at the time, compounding the sense of shame for both of us. Although he never wavered in his belief in me, it proved immensely challenging for him to endure the stares and whispers from his coworkers. Looking back, I consider this period one of the most demanding tests of our relationship. Without the foundation of trust, love, and faith in each other, I don't believe we could have weathered it.

But perhaps what impacted me the most was the thought of having my kids read the story on the Internet someday. That feeling was the hardest one to make peace with. What would I say? How would I explain? I spent the next few years living in fear of having my kids or people google my name and base their opinion of me on Internet gossip.

I entered a deep depression—one that filled my heart and soul with fear, self doubt, and shame. Resentment was also present, and I couldn't help but think that had my boss been a woman, our professional relationship would not have been in question. For the first time in my life, I truly understood the meaning of gender bias. It was as if being a woman automatically made me guilty of something I had not done.

Though it seemed like an impossible task, I was determined to prove to everyone who doubted me that they were wrong. I poured all my energy into my work, striving harder than ever before, and each promotion that came my way after that was all the sweeter. I wanted to say, "Look, it was my merit that got me here, nothing else."

The journey to rebuild my reputation and restore my confidence was a difficult one, but I was fortunate enough to find new opportunities within the company that allowed me a fresh start. I had to remind myself that I was not defined by the false allegations made against me and that my worth was not determined by the judgment of others.

As time passed, I slowly made peace with what had happened and accepted this chapter in my life as one that taught me resilience and strength. I learned to stand up to my fears and face the judgment head-on. This experience gave me the confidence to tackle other challenges in my life, knowing that no challenge could come close to the shame I felt when the story first went public. I have learned that everyone has their own story, their own struggles, and their own battles to fight.

It's how we deal with these challenges that define who we are as individuals. Looking back, I realize that the hardest part was not the story itself but finding the silver lining in a difficult situation.

It took me years to accept the harsh reality that the story would forever remain accessible online, and the toll it took on me seemed inconsequential to those responsible for the websites that posted it and the readers who consumed it. I had to make peace with it and change the narrative in my head. Overcoming this challenge was no easy feat; most people would have simply run away from it— continued to bury the story and live with the shame. But as I went through it, I started to view the incident and my ability to endure as something extraordinary, like having a superpower of bravery and resilience. It made me feel empowered, and I realized just how far I had come. I needed to be proud of myself for overcoming it, and that's the story I wanted my kids to take away.

Although we cannot dictate others' opinions of us, we hold the power to shape our own self-perception. Rather than attempting to change others' viewpoints, our focus should be directed toward our own actions. It is our actions that truly define us and influence how others perceive us. Regardless of the obstacles we encounter, there is always an opportunity for personal growth, each challenge serving as a stepping-stone toward strength and enlightenment. Through my own journey, I have realized that our inner strength and faith blossom in those moments when we believe we cannot go on, yet find a way.

Additionally, this experience has emphasized the significance of a strong support system, in both my personal and professional life. My husband's unwavering support served as a constant pillar of strength during this challenging period, and many of my colleagues' solidarity and encouragement inspired me to persevere.

Although time has passed, the lessons learned remain deeply ingrained in my being. As a mother, I strive to share these invaluable lessons with my children, empowering them to overcome any adversity they may encounter. Believe in your own resilience, for you are stronger than you realize.

ABOUT THE AUTHOR

SANDRA PANTOJA

At her core, Sandra Pantoja embodies the spirit of entrepreneurship. With a strong foundation in Corporate America, Sandra seamlessly balances her career with her true passion for real estate and business investments. Her most recent venture involves acquiring a charming European Bistro nestled in the beautiful Texas Hill Country. When she isn't immersed in her corporate job or managing her businesses, Sandra finds joy in exploring new culinary experiences and sharing a good meal in the company of friends and family. Sandra's fearless spirit pushes her to constantly challenge herself and embrace fresh opportunities as they arise. Connect with her on Instagram @sbpantoja

Chapter 6

RISE ABOVE YOUR CIRCUMSTANCES

Belinda Sandor

"Look inside,
that's where
your power lies."

From the time I was a little girl, I had a plan: go to college, get a job, get married, buy a home, have a baby or two, save money for retirement, and live happily ever after. It sounded like a simple plan, but it turned out it wasn't an easy plan.

My path started in Poughkeepsie, New York; then went to Mahopac, New York; Vienna, Virginia; Barrington, Illinois; and finally, New Canaan, Connecticut, where I graduated from high school. As an adult, I kept moving: Fort Worth, Texas; Ketchum, Idaho; Boise, Idaho; Vienna, Virginia; Charlottesville, Virginia; Belmont, Massachusetts; and Boston before I landed back in New Canaan, the place I now call home.

Moving so much skewed my view of the world. Because when you're in third grade, fifth grade, and ninth grade and leave your friends and favorite teachers behind, you start to think of friendships as temporary. Because, after all, I never knew when I might move again and start all over.

Some people thrive in that situation. I felt like I had no anchor.

Each town we lived in had a different culture, different activities, and different friend groups to break into. I found the process of getting acclimated to a new town agonizing. The first few weeks of school were always the worst; I'll never forget the feeling of dread while walking into the cafeteria alone and facing a sea of strangers.

I tried to make new friends; I wanted to fit in, and put a lot of pressure on myself. My clothes and hair were different, the way I talked was different, the kids were not forgiving, and some teased me. To most of them, I was invisible. Looking back, I realize that the sad thing was that I measured my self-worth by how they treated me. I gave a lot of power to people I didn't know, people who never saw me.

I kept the struggle to fit in under the radar until I started dating. That's when the real consequences began. I was a disaster at dating. Instead of considering what I wanted and what was important to me, I twisted myself around to fit into the life of each guy I went out with. I changed my clothes, my hair, my interests, and how I spent my time. I was a chameleon. Although I knew I was doing it, I didn't know why. But it drove me hard.

I realize now that what I sought in these relationships was relief—the relief of feeling accepted, loved, and knowing I belonged somewhere. I was desperate for it, and as sad as it is to remember, I would have done almost anything to have that feeling. If I could whisper in my young ear from my vantage point today, I would tell myself to look inside. That's where your power lies.

I managed to stay on track with the original plan. I finished college, got a job, bought a home, married, and had a baby girl named Emily. My path was not straight, but at least I was on it. I was hanging on for dear life.

From the outside, everything looked great. I remember posting a picture of my family on Facebook when Emily was seven. A friend commented that it was the kind of picture the manufacturer puts inside a frame so that you will buy it—a perfect family.

I knew deep inside that I was not in the right place. I went through the motions but felt alone and empty. I was deeply unhappy in my marriage. Emily's dad and I were not aligned in our parenting. We were not aligned financially. We were not aligned in our plans for the future. Despite this, I continued to twist myself, trying to make it work. But it kept getting worse for me, and eventually, I lost hope.

I started walking around the pond in my neighborhood for hours every day, grieving, and planning what would come next. Walking around my home, I imagined a future when only Emily and I would be living there. At the same time, the sadness that came from walking away from the person I thought I would build a life with was difficult to face. Because I was my family's primary breadwinner and mortgage owner, financial uncertainty added a layer of complexity, making my next steps even more difficult to take.

After Emily was born, I returned to my corporate job. It was a difficult choice for a forty-year-old first-time mother who wanted to find a way to work from home. The state of the world was making it urgent for me. It was October 2001, one month after 9/11.

I worked in the Prudential Tower, one of the tallest buildings in Boston and a potential target of another 9/11-style attack. Sitting in the dark with Emily every night, I worried about this possibility. To soothe myself, I kept running shoes in my office desk drawer to run the three miles home if something terrible happened.

Fortunately, I didn't have to worry for long. After six days back in the office, I was laid off. I went home, let the nanny go, wrote a business plan, and took the layoff as a sign. I would start my own business, working from home. I loved technology and was knee-deep in baby stuff. It made perfect sense to me to sell baby gifts online. I named my first business Blueberry Babies.

Although the business was successful in many ways, the financial piece was always stressful. Managing a company that relied on having inventory meant I would need more money than I'd thought. So I invested some of my savings and then started to rely on credit cards and loans to hold it together. Since sales increased every month, I kept thinking I was just one big month away from being able to make it work. That kept me hopeful, but it also blinded me. Blueberry Babies did not grow enough to support my family, no matter how hard I tried.

I kept my head down, trying to create success in Blueberry Babies for eight long years. I was constantly juggling my time between work and being a mother, juggling money and expenses and navigating my marriage that was holding on by a thread. I was exhausted all the time.

The business was failing, which meant there were personal financial consequences. Starting a new business and borrowing money relies on using personal credit, so even though "the business" had racked up all the debt, I was on the hook.

I had not paid the mortgage for over a year. I had blown through my savings and hadn't paid taxes in seven years. I had over six figures of debt and no income.

And I was about to turn fifty. I had always placed importance on the milestone of turning fifty. The big birthdays got my attention. The Big 3-0, the Big 4-0, and now the Big 5-0. According to the plan I'd made as I grew up, I had expectations: by thirty, be married; by forty, have a family and earn more than $100,000 a year.

This was the plan for fifty:

Happily married

Financially stable

Proud homeowner

Great job

Retirement savings underway

I asked myself how I had gotten so far away from the original plan. My desires had not changed. But my actions were working against me, and I didn't know why.

I had arrived at a crossroads. There was no more available credit and no more stalling the mortgage company, and the IRS was likely on my heels. I knew I had to make changes, big changes. But I was overwhelmed and out of ideas. I couldn't take the pressure anymore. I didn't want to deal with any of it.

Then one Saturday morning, I woke up, and I was different. I finally realized I did not have to be this unhappy and decided to get divorced. It felt like an enormous weight was lifted off my shoulders.

At that moment, I also realized I was still making decisions to fit in. Fit in with my friends and my community, fit in to hold a marriage together, fit in as a business owner, just like I had as a kid. I was still doing it. It had become second nature to me. It wasn't working, and I decided to stop.

I've got debt collectors calling me all day. I have seven years of back taxes to file and pay, I have to sell my home, I have no money, I don't have a job, and I'm acting like everything is okay. Nothing is okay.

I followed my instincts and pulled back from everything. I stopped spending time with my friends. I stopped spending time with my family. I stopped looking for a job. Instead, I decided to start spending time with myself. I quieted the noise around me to hear what I was thinking.

In a moment of clarity, I decided to think of the debt merely as numbers, remove the emotion, and create a strategy to win. As I did that, my energy changed a little at a time. I stopped thinking about my defeat and started thinking about taking back my life. I could live into that, I thought. *Game freaking on.*

I got into action. I sold my home and paid the liens that had been placed against it at the closing. I paid off the most threatening debts with the proceeds from the house, which relieved some of the pressure. I made a three-part plan:

1. Figure out how to make money.

2. Stop the growing interest on the credit card balances and pay them off.

3. File my back taxes and start a payment plan with the IRS.

I knew that a critical component of this plan was removing the judgment, emotions, and self-criticism running rampant in my head. It was simple but not easy. The voices in my head were relentless. When the chatter would start, I would say to myself, usually out loud, "Oh yeah, we're not doing this now," and replace the voices with something else. Sometimes it was listening to a self-help audiobook, and other times, it was country music. Eventually, I could guide my thoughts myself.

Plan Part One: Tackle Making Money

I was an administrative assistant in my twenties. Back then, we were called secretaries. I was naturally good at and liked this work, so I started working as an office temp for an agency to bring in money. It didn't pay well, but I was in the business world again, which felt like a big step.

Every morning, I walked Emily to the school bus stop and hung out with the dads waiting for the bus. One day one of the dads, Will, asked me what was new, and I told him that I was temping and thinking about starting a business offering admin services to entrepreneurs.

A grin covered his face as he told me he had left his job about a month before and started a business. He was drowning in administrative work and wanted some help. He asked if I would be interested in working with him. It was perfect. We knew and trusted each other, and he hired me.

My first client! I paid his bills, organized his email, set up QuickBooks, and ran errands for him. He was relieved, and I loved the work. And I loved getting paid.

I met my next client in the buffet line at a wedding reception. I was chatting with a man named Michael and his wife, Linda. Michael asked me about my work, and I told him I was doing admin work for a local entrepreneur. I explained that I wanted to turn it into a business.

He gave me his business card; I didn't have one yet, and I sent him a connection request on LinkedIn the next day.

It felt like such a bold move. I wondered if he might think I wanted something from him. Little did I know that making connections was how businesses succeed and that I would make many more.

A couple of weeks later, Michael sent me a message via LinkedIn asking if I could help him with an event he was hosting at a local company. I said yes—client number two.

I was learning a new way to work. Michael lived about an hour away, and although the event was in person, the planning was not. So instead of meeting in person, we talked on the phone and used screen-sharing software to collaborate. Working virtually with him opened my eyes. What if I didn't need to meet with my clients in person?

Michael's event was a success, and afterward, we grabbed a cup of tea. He told me he wanted to start offering webinars on the Internet and wondered if I would consider helping him set that up. He said he would pay me to figure it out if I was interested. I enjoyed working with him, so I said yes.

I was starting to think this was going to work—especially if clients would pay me to learn things for them. I could do that all day. I loved working on the computer, solving problems, and helping people. And I was getting paid.

Plan Part Two: Pay Off Credit Card Debt

I don't remember how many credit cards I had maxed out, but it's probably better that way. I knew it would help me see my progress as I paid them off, so I made a spreadsheet listing each card, the balance, and the date the payments were due. Then, I sorted the spreadsheet according to the amount owed and started paying off the cards with the smallest balance. To my profound disappointment, as I paid each account off, the bank closed it. I couldn't believe it. My first thought was that I was being penalized for being responsible, but it was a blessing not to have any credit. It forced me to stay the course.

Plan Part Three: Deal with Back Taxes

Unlike credit card debt, filing back taxes required me to wade through an unbelievable amount of paper. Seven years of bank statements for five bank accounts, seven years of credit card statements, and seven years of receipts packed in half a dozen banker's boxes that crowded my small apartment living room. They stayed there for a couple of years before I could face opening them.

Every day I saw the boxes, I felt ashamed and worried about the consequences of ignoring the taxes for so long. Friends tried to encourage me, but I couldn't bear to talk about it.

There was much more to the taxes than organizing paper; I knew I couldn't do this alone. I would need to find an accountant to help me. I had no idea how to prepare taxes for my business, Blueberry Babies, much less one that was taking a loss. An accountant would be expensive, and I would need thousands of dollars that I didn't have to pay them. The whole project paralyzed me.

One day, I'm not sure why, I picked up one of the boxes and set it on the dining room table. I lifted the lid, took the papers out, and scattered them on the table. Then, without looking at the details, I sorted them according to year. I then picked up a second box and did the same thing. I was careful not to read the pages. I knew that would be too much, and I would lose momentum.

I arranged the contents of all six boxes into seven mountains of paper. Seeing the stacks spread out inspired me to continue taking action, even though I was terrified to face the dollar amount I would owe when it was over. I kept going.

At about the same time I started the tax project, I began a relationship with a man I'd known in high school, my current husband, Greg, who was a certified public accountant. He painstakingly worked through every return with me and spent hours talking to the IRS on my behalf. Once I had filed all seven returns, I entered into a payment agreement with the IRS and started the years-long road to pay my back taxes. Although I owed almost $90,000, I felt enormous relief in no longer being a tax evader and constantly worrying about what might happen. It would take me seven years to pay that debt.

My business was thriving. I named it RocketGirl Solutions, built a website, got myself some business cards, and started writing an email newsletter to establish myself as a business owner and spread the word about my work. My clients were now all over the country and eventually would be worldwide.

The first year I was in business, I earned $70,000. For the next ten years, I made over $100,000 doing work I loved from home.

I had established myself as a virtual assistant working solely online, which was a blessing since Greg lived three hours away. The fact that I could now work from anywhere was much easier on our long-distance romance.

Staying the course allowed me to be the mom who could pick my daughter up from the bus stop, hold her hand while walking home, and hear all about her day. It allowed me to be the one to take care of her when she was sick. It allowed me to trust myself, my choices, and my judgment for the first time.

Over time, I reframed my life and built a new story as an emotionally self-reliant woman, including being a mom, a successful business owner, and, eventually, Greg's wife. For the first time in my adult life, I chose my partner according to the path I wanted my life to take and not by changing myself to fit into their desires. I created a list of values and attributes that would complement mine and didn't compromise.

After spending time with Greg for about a year, I sat down with him and shared my list, and we talked about our future together. It was a new kind of conversation for me. One where I could honestly articulate the plan I had put my life back on and the path I planned to stay on.

A couple of years later, when the time was right for us, Emily and I moved from Boston to New Canaan, where I had originally met Greg in high school in 1976, and we became a family.

I learned many lessons along the way:

Find your dream. I started with a plan, but as I became more grounded and trusted myself more, I allowed myself to dream. I'm now a gardener and chicken mama, and Greg and I are looking for a farm surrounded by rolling hills where we'll settle down. It's everything I've ever wanted.

Embrace discomfort. Starting a new business, blowing up a marriage, or making big changes is never easy or convenient. That's okay; just keep plugging away. You'll get there as long as you keep moving.

Teach the voices in your head to be kind when they speak to you. I've learned that you can't stop the voices from talking, but you can change what they say and how they say it. Replace the negative thoughts with something helpful, like audiobooks or your favorite music. I don't let them run the show.

Confidence is an inside job. Confidence, I discovered, is something you create yourself, not something that comes along or happens on its own. Don't wait until you've got the confidence to take action. If you want confidence, keep your word to yourself. Once you know you can trust yourself, your confidence will soar.

Stop worrying about what other people think of you. I read somewhere that attendance at your funeral largely depends on the weather. Think about that for a second when considering what someone thinks about your life and your choices.

Celebrate your successes—every single one. Celebrating has never been easy for me, but I took this on in earnest. I love high fives. I love the energy that happens when my hand meets Greg's, and I tell him a story of a new win.

And speaking of celebrating wins, I started a third business called The VA Connection in 2019. I teach women how to create and own thriving businesses as virtual assistants like me. After four short years, that business will have earned $1M. That from a woman who was once more than $100,000 in debt, jobless, and unable to pay her taxes.

I turned my life around. People who don't know me well might call me lucky. I have some great news. Luck has nothing to do with it. What's required is hard work, determination, focus, and listening to your heart.

I am at home in my business, at home in my marriage, and at peace in my heart. And after everything I had experienced, I learned that once I stopped trying to fit in, once I stopped caring what other people thought and started being myself, I could be at home anywhere. I would always be home.

ABOUT THE AUTHOR

BELINDA SANDOR

After more than a decade as a virtual assistant, Belinda Sandor founded The VA Connection®, an online community serving more than thirty thousand women in forty-seven countries where she coaches and mentors women to have their own successful businesses as VAs. With her relatable, down-to-earth style, Belinda guides women to build their confidence and do the work to achieve self-reliance. She has been quoted in *Inc.*, *The Wall Street Journal*, *The New York Times*, and *Parenting* magazine.

When she's not in the backyard with her chickens, Belinda can be found playing backgammon with her husband, Greg, or listening to country music with her daughter, Emily. To explore how you can build and grow a virtual assistant business, visit TheVAConnection.com

Chapter 7

EMERGE FROM THE FOG

JoAnne Dykhuizen

"Continue to pursue your dreams no matter what the odds."

I'm standing alone in the middle of a forest. It's evening, and I'm not able to remember how I got here or how long I've been standing here. The air is cold and damp, and it's making me shiver. I long for the comfort of my home and my dog, Tiny. The wolves, owls, and other creatures of the night begin their nighttime concert, which frightens me. I cry and scream, but no one hears me. I'm afraid to move. I am lost, confused, alone, and eight and a half years old.

Where is my family? Will I ever escape this bad dream?

My best childhood memories are of getting together with family at my maternal grandparents' apartment. My mom came from a large family, and I looked forward to seeing all my aunts, uncles, and cousins each week. But the one thing that separated me from the rest of the cousins was that I was an only child. That would prove to be a huge factor throughout my childhood.

My happy childhood crumbled into pieces with the loss of my maternal grandparents two weeks apart when I was eight and a half. How would I go on without them in my life? They were everything to me. I had spent a lot of time with them, especially since we lived above them in a duplex apartment building. Many of the emotions I felt in my dreams reflected what I was experiencing while I was awake. I was so traumatized by their loss that when I try to recall the first three years after their death, I can remember only fragments. To this day, I am sad about the fact that I was so young when my grandparents died. As I grew older, I thought of many questions I wish I'd been able to ask them and many things I wanted to talk with them about. But there hadn't been enough time. I don't think my parents ever talked to me about my grief or theirs, because back then, people didn't talk about their feelings as openly as they do now. I knew, though, that I would never be the same and would never again experience the happy childhood that I'd once had.

I'm thankful that I'll always have those memories. My family continued to visit each other occasionally, but eventually the get-togethers would be few and far between, and then we would see each other only at weddings or funerals. It wasn't until recently that my cousins and I started getting together once a year for a cousins reunion. I'm thrilled to see family members again, though some of them are no longer with us.

Fortunately, my parents and grandparents had dogs throughout my childhood. Dogs are still an important part of my life. Even though I can't remember, in my heart I know the dogs were a huge source of comfort to me during those three years when I was grieving. They were my best friends.

By the time I came out of the foggy darkness I had been living in for three years, I had changed: Gone were the feelings of safety, protection, and happiness, and my outgoing personality. They were replaced with insecurity, anxiety, and shyness. I had somehow built a brick wall around my heart that would take years to melt away. I was afraid of letting people get too close to me, because I couldn't bear the thought of losing someone close to me again. Nonetheless, I would have to bear many more losses throughout my adult life.

When I was nineteen, I started traveling to California to visit friends several times a year. Unfortunately, I also started experiencing panic attacks on a regular basis. The first one happened on a freeway, and I was terrified. I couldn't breathe, and then I started to shake and tremble. My attacks became so severe that I didn't want to drive. The thought of driving over a bridge or on a freeway or expressway would trigger a panic attack. It was paralyzing. This went on for decades. I was prescribed medications, some of which were so strong, I couldn't even function. I finally decided to take matters into my own hands and took some classes to learn techniques that would help lessen the frequency of the attacks without the use of medications. I also had several sessions with a psychologist. I was not going to live my life like that anymore. I was missing out on so many things.

As soon as I had my panic attacks under control (or so I thought), I decided to move to California. A few years later, I returned to Chicago and met and married my husband, John. Before I met John, he was involved in auto racing, which I knew very little about. John took me to my first auto race in Milwaukee, and I was immediately in love with it. We traveled several times a year to races throughout the country. Little did I realize at the time that those next twenty-three years would include some of the happiest and most memorable times in my life.

My mom's diagnosis of osteosarcoma, a type of bone cancer, was another huge loss for me. My mom was the bravest person I had ever known. She had such a positive outlook about her diagnosis and refused to give up until the chemo treatments became too difficult for her to continue.

A year later, John received a diagnosis of multiple sclerosis (MS). He was in and out of the hospital throughout his seven-year illness, three years of which he was bedridden at home. Although I had helped my dad in his caregiving responsibilities for my mom in a small capacity, it didn't prepare me at all for taking care of John. It was challenging and heartbreaking, seeing the person I loved suffering from this debilitating illness. We hired home health care for him during the day while I worked, and I was there after work and on weekends. Long-term care insurance was not an option for the first few years, and when it became available, we were turned down. John had a preexisting condition, so we had to pay for home health care from our savings account. I was also visiting my dad every weekend as well as helping him financially.

Those seven years took a toll on both of us, but I was determined to keep him at home rather than put him in a nursing home. I knew that would destroy him. As long as he felt comfortable at home, and his quality of life was still good, that's what I was going to do for him, no matter what it took. The week that John died, I didn't know where our next meals were going to come from, and we were $86,000 in debt. Fortunately, we both had life insurance policies, and I was able to pay most of the bills from his policy. We were maxed out on our credit cards, and it took several years to pay them off.

I spent half of my working life as a legal secretary for a law firm in downtown Chicago. It was a great place to work, and I loved working there. The camaraderie between the attorneys, legal secretaries, and staff was extraordinary. The respect and appreciation from the attorneys for the hard work that each of us contributed made it a great working environment.

I was eventually given the opportunity for a management position, which I was really excited about. However, going from legal secretary to a management position proved to be difficult for me. Unfortunately, it became quite evident after a few months that my views and management's views were not compatible, which resulted in my going back to being a legal secretary.

A CEO was hired from outside the firm, and that's when things slowly started taking a turn for the worse. It was also becoming quite a toxic environment. My panic attacks returned because of the stress of John's illness and not knowing from one day to the next whether I would have a job tomorrow. These attacks were much more intense than previous episodes, including one that required me to be driven by ambulance from work to a local hospital. The paramedics described it as a hypertension crisis, which was life threatening.

One of the attorneys I was working for was extremely demanding, but I kept working for her because I needed the job. I really had no choice at that time in my life, because John continued to need home health care, we needed the insurance, and I needed to work to pay the bills that had rapidly depleted our savings account. It was not the kind of situation that I wanted to be in at all. I felt trapped and couldn't do anything about it. The attorney for whom I worked was always trying to drag me down with her hurtful and condescending remarks, saying I "wasn't the best secretary at the firm" or giving me a bad merit review when John was ill, saying that I wasn't performing "up to par."

Those words stung, especially because although it would have been covered under the Family Leave Act, I didn't take one day off during John's illness. I was told by human resources that if I didn't improve my work, I would receive a lower bonus that next year. To make matters worse, I had fractured my foot and was in a boot for several weeks. Trying to navigate taking the train downtown every day on crutches proved to be quite an experience. My boss's callousness was appalling and made me extremely angry, but it was a blessing in disguise: she was unknowingly instrumental in helping me make a big decision I had been putting off. After John died, and once I could think clearly again, I decided that I didn't want to live that way anymore and no longer wanted to put up with my boss's condescending comments. I didn't deserve to be treated that way and wasn't going to put up with it any longer. I was able to take back control of my life, and it felt great! It was then that I decided to leave on my own and on my own terms. But before making such a move, I needed to get things in order. The day finally arrived, and on April 30, 2014, I left the law firm and corporate America for the last time.

Despite all the challenges, choosing to leave a law firm in corporate America after thirty-five years was truly one of the hardest decisions I've ever had to make. I had invested so much time at the firm, and it was difficult to come out of my comfort zone. In reality, it was also the best decision I ever made. Leaving a high-paying job to start my own business was both scary and exciting at the same time. Exciting because now I finally had the chance to branch out as an entrepreneur as a canine massage therapist. The vision of being my own boss was empowering! Scary because canine massage was a relatively new business, like in the pioneer stages, and most pet owners had never heard of it. But I wanted to do it in honor of my golden retriever, Duke, my dad's dog, Patches (who came to live with Duke and me for seven years after my dad's death), and all the other dogs in my life growing up, who were a great source of comfort to me in so many ways during major losses.

While I was still working at the law firm, I attended canine massage classes on Sundays. Unfortunately, Duke had passed three months before the classes started, and the first day, we had to go around the room, introduce ourselves, and tell the group why we were taking canine massage classes. When it was my turn, I burst into tears and couldn't even get words out of my mouth. I'll always remember the empathy my classmates showed me. Duke was another great loss in my life as well as Patches a few years later. Those who have suffered the loss of a dog know how devastating it is. Throughout the classes, we continued to show support for each other.

I thought the canine massage classes would be easy for me since I'd had dogs through most of my life. What a humbling experience it turned out to be. I discovered that I knew absolutely nothing about dogs. The classes were intensive. Learning canine anatomy, physiology, and kinesiology proved to be difficult for me, but once again my classmates came to my rescue and helped me get through some tough lessons.

Before I decided to go to canine massage school, I volunteered at a shelter in my area. On my first day as a volunteer, I was assigned the Stray Room, where stray dogs or owner give-ups are automatically quarantined for two weeks until they are seen by a vet or because they need other special attention. As I entered the room the first time, I saw the look in many of the dogs' eyes and the sadness and loneliness in them. Some were shaking so much that you just wanted to hold them and tell them they were loved. The dogs seemed confused, as if they didn't know what had happened or why they were there. No one could give them the answers they wanted to hear, either. They were in this strange, frightening place where they didn't know anyone and were alone.

You could tell that many of them were experiencing the loss of comfort, safety, protection, and happiness. It tore at my heartstrings because I could totally relate to what they were going through: I had gone through the same experiences and emotions after the loss of my grandparents, my mom, my dad, and John.

After walking the dogs, we were able to spend time with the ones that needed a little extra TLC. I would always pick the one that I felt needed the most love and attention. I would hold them, gently massage them, tell them they were loved, and just spend quality time with them. I saw that canine massage really helped relieve their anxiety, tension, and stress. When I left the shelter after every shift, I would say a prayer that all the animals there would feel loved and would be adopted quickly.

As soon as I graduated from canine massage school, I thought I would have a lot of clients because I knew that canine massage would be beneficial to all dogs. I had none. I couldn't understand why, and it was a huge disappointment. What I discovered is that the majority of dog owners have never heard of canine massage or its value and benefits to their dogs. It breaks my heart when I see a dog who could really benefit from canine massage but whose owner does not understand its real advantages and worth. On the other hand, I love seeing the joy on pet parents' faces when they see that massage is so helpful. Although canine massage therapists do not diagnose, we work with vets to develop a plan that works best for the dog and their pet parents.

I started doing speaking presentations and podcasts. Because dogs had played such an important part in my life, it was my turn to do whatever I could to share the knowledge and experience I'd gained since 2013 so people's dogs could live a healthier and happier lifestyle. It's never too late to take a proactive approach with your dog, no matter what their age is. I would meet people at pet events and get calls two or three years later because their dog(s) were having severe issues or I was their last resort when they had tried everything else.

I found out that there is definitely a learning curve between being an employee in corporate America and becoming an entrepreneur. A lot of trials and errors. To say that the first several years of my canine massage business were very discouraging is an understatement. I definitely wasn't an overnight success! Several times I decided to close down and move on to something else. But every time I wanted to give up, something would happen that would direct me back to canine massage. I would remember dogs I had helped in the past and knew that if I just called it quits, I wouldn't be able to help other dogs who might need my help. So, despite all the odds, I have continued with my practice, and now I do canine massages, speaking presentations, podcasts, blogs, and other educational programs.

Dogs have had a healing effect on me throughout my life, and whenever I see dogs respond positively to canine massage and the joy on their owners' faces, I know that this has always been my purpose in life; it just took me a long time to realize it. I have the best job in the world!

Like the majority of us, I've faced many disappointments, major losses, and other challenges, but my friends and family have helped me know I'm not alone, work through my grief, and appreciate all the wonderful memories I've made along the way. My journey and experiences have also helped me develop strength and independence and the option of making my own choices. I've learned never to give up, to continue to pursue your dreams no matter what the odds. I don't want to leave any more regrets on my plate. My dogs have also been great teachers. They've taught me how to open my heart to love and happiness.

ABOUT THE AUTHOR

JOANNE DYKHUIZEN

JoAnne Dykhuizen doesn't just love dogs, she also wants to help them live healthier and happier lives. She travels all over Illinois and beyond as a certified canine massage therapist and the Owner of Feel So Good Canine Massage, LLC. JoAnne presents workshops on topics like "The Conversation You Wish You Could Have With Your Dog" and "Snap, Crackle, Pop – Canine Arthritis" to help pet owners and dog lovers keep their canine companions healthy and happy. When she's not working with pets and their people, you can find her exploring the natural wonders of the western United States. To book her for your next event or podcast visit, please contact her at: https: www.feelsogoodk9massage.com

Chapter 8

SCALE THE MOUNTAIN

Marcia Murff Tabor

"I will climb on because I know I can."

Tick, tick, tick . . . *Am I going crazy?* Tick, tick, tick . . . *I must be going crazy.* Tick, tick, tick . . . *I can't get enough air. I can't breathe.* Tick, tick, tick . . . *I feel like I can't swallow.* Tick, tick, tick . . . *I can't stand the sound of this clock! Why is time passing by so slowly? When will this feeling ever end? Will it end? Will I be like this forever? Oh God. Dear God. Why me, God? What is happening? I don't know what is happening. I must be going crazy. That's the only explanation.*

I lived a normal life as a normal teenager in a normal small town until suddenly, I was paralyzed by panic attacks. At the age of nineteen, I was a happy-go-lucky college student, and then I wasn't. I left after the fall semester of my sophomore year, debilitated by something I didn't know or understand. My parents were at a loss. I think we were all secretly worried about our worst fears of madness. My grandfather had been given a diagnosis of schizophrenia at age forty.

Was I going crazy, too?

I started feeling a little better and decided to see if I could go back to work at Hardee's, the fastfood place where I worked in high school. I was desperate to get out of the house and yet oh so worried I would have one of those attacks even though I had no idea what was happening to me. I lasted a week. I was working when it felt like Mike Tyson planted a firm upper cut across my face. Everything was spinning. I couldn't focus. My depth perception was off, my hands were shaking, my heart was racing, I felt as though I couldn't swallow, and I was hyperventilating. I was gripping the counter like it was a life raft on the *Titanic*.

My mother was a teacher, and it was a school day, so they called my father. My sweet daddy walked into Hardee's, came behind the counter, scooped me up in his arms like a small child, and carried me home. I never returned. That Hardee's is no longer standing, but I see the spot where it was when I drive home to visit my mom, and instantly recall those feelings.

After that, I didn't leave my parents' house for more than a month. Just walking out to the driveway seemed too scary. I lay in my bed or sat on the couch. It was the beginning days of MTV, and I watched it on a loop. Even with the TV blaring, I could still hear the clock ticking in my parents' den. A ticking clock is a trigger to this day.

My mother took me to get my blood sugar tested . . . perfect. My mother took me to get my heart tested . . . also perfect. My mother took me to an allergist who performed a series of skin tests . . . again, perfect. Now more convinced than ever,

I thought, *I am going mad, crazy, cuckoo. I don't think I can live this way. I am surviving by the minute.*

Sometimes people describe panic attacks as a moment. Maybe a short moment or maybe a long moment but a moment. My panic attacks came in waves that never truly subsided and lasted for weeks to months. And the ticking clock always reminded me just how long a second, ten seconds, thirty seconds, a minute, a half hour, an hour, a day, a night could feel.

One of those nights I was completely inside myself, feeling every gasp of breath that wasn't quite enough, feeling every swallow I struggled to complete, feeling disoriented, feeling exhausted and yet shaking anxiously, feeling dizzy as though the floor were moving beneath my feet, feeling as though I wanted to escape but what I wanted to escape from was myself, my own body. My mother was cooking dinner and called my father, my brother, and me to come to the table. I frantically started walking circles around the den, living room, and kitchen and back, over and over. "I can't breathe," I said. "I can't breathe!" I walked faster and faster and repeated myself. "I can't breathe! Help me."

By this point, my parents were exasperated. I looked fine. What in the world could be wrong? Was I just being dramatic? The moment is seared in my memory bank for life. My dear parents loaded me into the car. I had the window down, trying to get more air into my lungs. They took me to an urgent-care center. I walked from one end of the waiting room to the other and back, over and over. I went to the window at reception every minute or so and told them I was desperate, I felt like I was dying. Once we got called back to see a doctor, he talked to us and then injected me with a sedative. My body, which had been as tense as being in a room full of poisonous snakes, instantly relaxed. The doctor told my mother he saw this occasionally in young people but offered no relief, no diagnosis. I find this to be most frightening: knowing something is wrong with you and yet no one being able to tell you what it is.

In the following months, the panic attacks started to subside. I ventured out of the house. I reenrolled in college (closer to home). I auditioned for a play, got a part, and performed. I performed in several plays. I got a job as a server while going to school and started performing singing telegrams for a family-owned business. Lisa, the woman who owned the singing telegram business, and her family were like a second family while I was in college.

Everything was going great until suddenly, it wasn't. Lisa called me one day to do a clown telegram and I was lying on the floor of my apartment, the panic consuming every crevice of my body. "I don't think I can do that today," I said. I explained that I was dizzy, that I couldn't catch my breath, that my heart was racing, that my hands were tingling, that I was unsteady on my feet because I felt like I was walking on a swinging bridge.

"Okay, Marcia," Lisa said. "I'm going to come and pick you up. You don't have to do the telegram. I'm just going to come and get you so you are not alone." Here I was, back at the bottom of the mountain. It was as if I had reached the top and jumped off the ledge, landing back at the bottom, not dead but wishing I was. Lisa's friend Paula was a licensed therapist, and Lisa asked her if she could see me. The day after Lisa picked me up during that panic episode, she took me to see Paula. We met for an hour while I described to her what I was experiencing. At the end of the session, Paula handed me a VHS tape of the *Phil Donahue Show* and told me to go home and watch it and return the following week.

The experts on the show listed and described thirteen symptoms: sweating; pounding heart; trembling or shaking; sensations of shortness of breath or feeling smothered; feelings of choking; chest discomfort; abdominal distress; feeling dizzy, light-headed, unsteady, or faint; sensations of heat or chills; paresthesia (numbness or tingling sensations); derealization (feelings of unreality) or depersonalization (feeling detached from oneself); fear of losing control or "going crazy"; and fear of dying.

The people on the taped show used the term *panic attack*. *Yes! This is it*, I thought. Finally, I was relieved. What was happening to me had a name. But then I learned that there is no cure.

As had happened before, this period of panic attack episodes lasted for some weeks and eventually subsided. Now that it had happened again, I had a palpable fear of its return. Afraid to do anything that might incite those feelings, I started avoiding places that might make it happen again. I avoided the mall, crowded places, and driving or walking far from my house or my car. I was willingly and purposely incarcerating myself with this faceless villain that was slowly taking over my thoughts and fears and, more than anything, paralyzing me with worry about the unknown. The unknown could be wondering if I could walk around the block without having a panic attack, if I could drive ten miles without having a panic attack, or if I could walk into the mall to the stores I had once frequented without having a panic attack.

Sometimes just thinking about those questions could bring about some of the symptoms. Here I was, down at the bottom of my internal Mount Everest, questioning if I would ever make it to base camp. The thought of making the summit to normalcy seemed so far out of reach, I couldn't even bring myself to imagine it.

I married my first husband and took my first professional job out of college. Again, I was on an upswing. I got pregnant and had my first child, my son. I was driving forty minutes down a busy interstate to get to work every day. Major strides, right? Of course! Did I still have panic attacks during these periods? Absolutely, but they weren't major, debilitating episodes. I remember traveling with my husband and infant to visit my parents, who lived about forty-five minutes away. On the way back home, I started feeling like I was gasping for air, then struggling to swallow. I told my husband I needed for him to stop at a convenience store because I needed some water. He said, "You can wait until we get home."

To this day, I do not leave my house without at least a bottle of water. Most of the time I have a case of water in my car. In airports, I have my bottle of water and, because I've had it taken at security before, carry several bottles of water in travel-size containers. Not being able to carry that bottle of water through security until I can get more brings about those feelings of panic. Once, in the Denver airport, I relinquished my water before going through security, and then, my current husband said we had to get on the tram to the next terminal. The anxiety on my face was apparent to him. He promised me it would be okay and that we would be on the train only a couple of minutes. It was the longest two minutes of my life and is the reason I now carry travel size water bottles that I can get through airport security.

That is what happens with panic attacks. Whatever has made you panic in the past is always a trigger in the future.

During my first professional job, I had just started my fifth year with the company and been awarded Employee of the Year when they sent me, along with another woman, to Minneapolis, Minnesota, for some software training. Again, all was well until it wasn't. Jan and I had finished a couple of days' training when we decided to go see the famous Mall of America. I remember walking in and seeing the Ferris wheel ahead. It was overwhelmingly large. Jan and I walked into a store, and as she was perusing the merchandise, I started feeling hot, a smothering hot feeling. It was coming. I knew it was coming. I managed to say to Jan, "I need to get out of here."

"Okay," she said. "I'm checking out, and then we can go." But it was already too late. I hadn't realized how well I had been doing the last few years. I had made it to base camp, and maybe I had even begun the summit when I plummeted. I fell below sea level. I fell into the valley. Here I was in Minnesota, in the winter, in the worst panic attack of my life, and I was supposed to get on a plane the next day. I was in a terrible nightmare. Imagine, if you will, me in a training with people who had seen me there for the last two days. I returned for the third day of training before we were to head to the airport but was unable to participate and couldn't think of anything other than worrying about how I could possibly walk through the airport, much less get on an airplane to get home. I had not slept the night before because after leaving the mall I could not get a full breath of air.

Jan got me through that day and through the airport and home. I know it had an impact on her, because when I saw her recently, she said she would never forget it. Once home, I was unable to return to work for more than two weeks. A kind coworker, Judy, drove across town twenty minutes out of her way to pick me up for work and take me home for at least another two weeks. I went to see another therapist and tried medication. It made me feel terrible. Despite panic attacks, I had the happy gene, and anti-anxiety meds and antidepressants messed with my happy gene. I had to fight this battle with my own will. I felt like a tiny speck on a mountain, a climber, and my panic attacks were the avalanche.

If I had to describe a person suffering from panic attacks to those who have never suffered from them, I would describe a person who seemed normal on the outside even while experiencing some of the symptoms. But imagine the person encased in a transparent tube of water on the inside. They are screaming, yet you can't hear them. They are wild-eyed with fear, yet you don't understand why. Imagine this person is running out of air, gasping and taking in water, although this is not what you see happening . . . The avalanche. Trapped inside the avalanche. How to ever escape?

At the time I took my greatest fall off the ledge, when I fell past all my other falls and landed in the valley where it was darkest, it felt as though I had been buried alive by this unstoppable avalanche of panic. At that moment, I was in great despair, but it is important for me to say to myself, *I didn't die. I survived, In fact, I thrived.* I have had more falls since then, but each subsequent fall is not as far as the previous one. I am making my way up the summit, but it is not a straight climb. It is climbing and then falling and getting back up and climbing and not falling as far the next time.

The fear of the panic attacks is still there, but how I deal with that fear has changed. I struck a match, an imaginary match. I looked inside this pit, this place where a person gets buried in an avalanche. If you don't dig your way out, you die. I held up the lit match to every corner and tried to learn and understand how I might escape. I fought this unpredictable nemesis with my own willpower even though many times I felt as though I had no willpower at all. In my quest to understand how to dig my way to the surface, I unmasked myself. I talked to people. I stripped away the fear of people's opinions and shared my mental anguish. My

happy gene made it impossible for many people to understand that I could suffer from a mental illness yet also smile
and be happy. Most of them could not reconcile the two.

I was not going to take medication. There was no easy fix.
I did not want to die under the weight of this avalanche
before digging out. I did not want it to take me with it. I had
to fight to escape this thing. But how? I fought it one block
at a time, one mile at a time, one step through a mall at a
time. I spent a decade taking tiny steps toward digging my
way out before the avalanche of panic could suck the last
air from my lungs.

There were moments like needing to drive my daughter to
an ocean-side camp in Charleston, South Carolina, but
knowing I had to drive back by myself riddled the trip with
anxiety. Once I returned from the trip, I felt so proud of
myself. However, even two or three years after that, I still
could not walk through a mall with her. I would drive her
to the entrance of a store she wanted to go to and then
make her get back in the car so I could drive to a different
entrance for another store. At home, I would walk down the
street until I could not see my house and then turn back,
and then the next week, I would make myself walk two more
driveways down and turn back. The feelings of panic would
be ever present, but I would have a continuous conversation
in my head about going just a little farther each time.

I remember going alone into a mall unfamiliar to me. Once
inside, I felt those feelings brimming beneath the surface.
Again, I had that same ongoing conversation with myself.

Although I was suffering terribly with this gripping and absurd fear of walking through the mall, I made myself take one step and then another. Making it through that mall was a monumental breakthrough. My steps toward less severe panic attacks have been incremental. At the time, they seemed small and inconsequential, but now, looking over years' worth of struggle, I see that they amount to my summit, my Mount Everest.

Most of my breakthroughs on panic attacks since then have come through my quest for knowledge about menopause. I started seeking cures for symptoms, and many of them had a positive impact on my panic attacks. I went to an acupuncturist who practices pre-Cold War Chinese acupuncture. He told me he did not treat specific symptoms but just reset the body's meridian. I went to him several times before I noticed that my anxiety had greatly diminished. I was calm. I was not having these thoughts of panic or triggers. I realized that he had reset my body to its intended balance, and the effect on my panic attacks was astonishing!

I went to see a woman who helped me with yoga-style stretching. She shared with me that "legs up the wall" helps your parasympathetic system settle. It was so hard at first. She would have me lie there with my legs up the wall for five to ten minutes. The first couple of minutes she would tell me to focus on my breathing. I just wanted to get up because I would find myself struggling to breathe, and yet if I remained in the position, the feeling would eventually subside.

I found my way to an amazing physical therapist who has taught me so much. She taught me to lie on a foam roller parallel to my spine and do chest openers. My shoulders are rounded to the front, and I believe that years of closing myself off in a protective mode from the panic attacks has negatively affected my posture. If I don't do these foam roller stretches, it could diminish my lung capacity in the years ahead, which could impact my panic attacks. She also taught me that anxiety and panic stems from the vagus nerve, and she has manipulated it on occasion.

I made a friend in recent years who taught yoga. She really trained me to do deep breathing. I had spent my entire life mostly shallow breathing from my chest, but I've learned to expand from the abdomen, the area around the ribs, the diaphragm, and lastly, the lungs.

I learned that as my anxiety grows, I raise my shoulders toward my ears. I now recognize when it is happening and pull my shoulders down and away from my ears and take those deep breaths. I have learned that meditation is powerful. We must take time in silence to listen to our inner selves. Meditation consists of stillness, breathing, and clearing your mind.

I have learned that deficiencies in vitamins and trace minerals can sometimes affect whether I am more vulnerable to a panic attack. I was found to be deficient in B vitamins. This can contribute to anxiety. If I don't take magnesium regularly, I can begin to have those anxious feelings at night.

It's been thirty-eight years since that first attack. When I look at my life, I see that I have succeeded in my career and with my family. I have done and experienced and participated in so much, yet I consider my greatest accomplishment the following: Where I used to stick close to home, I can now walk miles and miles . . . alone, drive to other states . . . alone, fly anywhere in the world . . . alone, walk through the mall, and push myself athletically where I used to stop when my heart rate increased to the point of having that panic feeling. Panic attacks have been my personal Mount Everest. I may have to climb this mountain again and again, but I have staked my flag at the top. In the last handful of years I have felt the sensation of being free, and if it happens again, I will climb on, because now I know I can.

ABOUT THE AUTHOR

MARCIA
MURFF TABOR

Marcia Murff Tabor has spent her life telling stories as a public relations manager. It wasn't until after she retired that she finally felt free to share her own. Her friends may know her from her days in theater or as a mom or a PR professional. Maybe they've heard some of her personal exploits like when she died on the table during a colonoscopy, or her three marriages, or the fact she's had so many car accidents she can't count them all but few know of her private struggle with panic attacks. Now she wants to share her story to help others fight the terror of panic and find their peace again. Follow her story . . . start a conversation . . . or share your story at @now_that_marcia_mentions_it on Instagram and TikTok or head to the website, www.nowthatmarciamentionsit.com

Chapter 9

JOURNEY TOWARD RESTORATION

Jill Ore

"Storms of life
are unpredictable."

Our first attempt to reach the lighthouse to open it for the 2022 summer season of restoration work was turned back by storms. We had set out on the water for this offshore location in northern Lake Michigan thinking we could avoid the approaching weather by navigating south, but weather and storms on the Great Lakes are unpredictable. The storms tracked south and found us!

We sought refuge by anchoring in the bay bordered by Wilderness State Park, waiting for the storms to pass. Seven of us huddled together under a tarp in a thirty-foot boat as the wind and rain delivered what we were trying to steer clear of. After six hours on the water, wet and running out of daylight, we returned to the marina. The empty lighthouse would withstand this day's storms as she had for over a century and await our arrival the following day. And I, at the start of my second year as head lighthouse keeper of White Shoal Light, would contemplate our shared resilience and journey toward restoration.

Storms of life are unpredictable—the kind brewed up by Mother Nature and the non-meteorological ones. I remember as a young girl being ushered into the basement with my sisters when gathering clouds or sirens signaled an approaching storm. As we sheltered together, clutching pillows and blankets, I would occasionally peek out the southwest window well, searching the skies for a funnel cloud or to catch a glimpse of the trees bending in the wind and the rain pouring down. Though to this day I have yet to witness a single tornado, growing up, I had recurring dreams of being in the basement just like that—huddling, waiting, and watching.

When the storms of life visit, is it possible to hide from them? Are there tarps wide and strong enough to hide under or basements deep enough to seek shelter in? By storms of life, I am talking about the personal kind—a trusted coach making unwanted advances, going through divorce, and becoming an empty nester. These storms can arrive unexpectedly or may be looming large on the horizon. My storms seemed to blow in to test me and find out what I was made of.

My early experience with these storms caused me to dim my light. I silenced my voice. I turned inward. If I could have been invisible, I would have chosen that. I shared very little or nothing of what was really happening in my life with anyone. I took it upon myself to bear the pain, the shame, and the uncertainty alone. I equated my silence with the appearance of success. If I could singly and silently navigate these turbulent waters, it would give the impression that the girl voted Most Likely to Succeed in high school was living up to that expectation.

How and who would I tell that my coach had made an unwanted personal advance toward me? I didn't want to reveal it to my parents, nor did I want to stir up a scandal in the community. Turning inward, I questioned whether I had done something to invite this attention. Those who perpetrate such deeds count on the silence of their targets, and I gave my coach no reason to doubt that my reaction would be any different. I never contemplated the effect my silence might have if he directed the same kind of behavior at someone else. I would eventually learn that I was not the only one hiding such a secret, but no one was speaking up.

I had to weigh whether my coming forward would jeopardize my position on the team. I weighed. I measured. I remained quiet. That was the beginning of my standing in a posture of resilience with a habit of silence. Alone I stood, weathering the storm in isolation and giving the outward appearance of normalcy.

Later, I carried this habit of silence into my marriage, when I chose to let small matters of disagreement remain unspoken. Why would I rock the boat over something so trivial? Being silent about the little stuff opened the door to rationalize remaining quiet about the bigger issues. I married someone who had been married before, so I paid attention to what he shared about the areas of conflict that ended that marriage. Wouldn't our divisions end in divorce as well?

My desire to steer clear of arguments in the name of keeping the peace was really an unsuccessful attempt at trying to control an outcome. Ten years of finding ways to justify keeping my true feelings hidden resulted in tension and strife anyway. The result I feared—divorce—was the result that came to pass, accompanied by swirling uncertainty: not knowing where I would land. Lives torn apart and scattered. That is yours. This is mine. The concept of "ours" was ripped apart. In a way, I was in the tornado I had always feared, and there was nowhere to hide.

How and when would I find my voice again? I barely confided in anyone when we decided to divorce. I reluctantly shared the news with my family but told no one at work until my boss approached me out of concern about how quiet and withdrawn I had become. Because I could scarcely utter the words "I am getting divorced," I carried on as if my life were normal. I wanted my son, Brian, to see I was keeping it together—standing stalwart and strong.

During a mission trip with Brian four years after the divorce, I was invited (maybe even called out a little) to share my thoughts with our Bible study group that gathered at the end of work each day. I had listened silently as everyone shared their stories and struggles, hoping no one would notice me. My strategy of remaining essentially an invisible observer was exposed. Time for me to find my voice.

The exact topic we were discussing that day escapes me now, but I do remember what I talked about to our study group, composed of eighth-grade students as well as other parent and teacher chaperones. I finally opened up about my divorce—what an incredible sense of failure I felt and how much I missed Brian on the days and nights he was at his dad's. As a mom, I had been unprepared for that separation, and I struggled with the realization there would be parts of my son's growing up that I would miss or be excluded from.

Beyond that, I could still recall the look on Brian's face when his dad and I sat him down four years earlier and told him we were divorcing. My sense of failure was deepened the day Brian's dad and I met with the counselor Brian was required to speak with during the divorce process. She shared with us that Brian was unable to speak with her at all about what he was feeling or how he was doing. Instead, his voice was the tears he cried during their time together. To uncover the depth and range of his emotions, she had asked Brian to draw her a picture of himself holding an umbrella in a rainy-day scene, with raindrops falling from the sky. Expressed through the picture, his vulnerability and sadness were magnified. The umbrella was small, meaning it wasn't protecting him from the really large raindrops falling from above. The large raindrops represented his fears, his sadness, his helplessness, and the weight of it all, which he was feeling but couldn't verbalize. Hearing the counselor's explanation of Brian's picture devastated me.

As my voice quivered and tears welled up in my eyes while sharing this story with the Bible study group, Brian left where he was sitting on the picnic table to come over and wrap his arms around me. He had never heard me speak about this. No one had. Not even me. Not out loud, anyway, and somehow, I survived the telling of it.

The last thing I shared with our study group were some Bible verses that had come to mean a lot to me during my divorce. Light as truth is often symbolized by a lighthouse. Turning to the Word of God while going through my divorce was that light for me. The words gave me understanding. This verse was illuminated to me while reading the Psalms repeatedly during that time:

> *Your road led through the sea,*
> *Your pathway through the mighty waters—*
> *A pathway no one knew was there*!

Psalm 77:19 (New Living Translation)

I questioned the purpose of everything I was going through. Was *through* really the best and only option? My prayer wasn't to continue to go through it. I was begging God to deliver me from it—go around, over, under, avoid—anything but through it. Then I remembered these verses:

> *"My thoughts are nothing like*
> *your thoughts," says the Lord.*
> *"And my ways are far beyond*
> *anything you could imagine.*
> *For just as the heavens are higher than*
> *the earth, so my ways are higher than your*
> *ways and my thoughts higher than your thoughts."*

Isaiah 55:8-9 (NLT)

I had to trust and believe that what God intended in leading me through this storm, even though I couldn't see it, would ultimately be for my good, my growth, and my refinement, and provide a path to restoration. Someday this would all make sense.

The uncertainty of where we would live and my ability to take care of a house all by myself would be answered when the tempest-tossed waters of my divorce settled, and I found my new home on a street called Stillwater Circle, fulfilling the promise in this passage:

The Lord is my shepherd; I shall not want.
He maketh me to lie down in green pastures;
He leadeth me beside the still waters.
He restoreth my soul.

Psalm 23:1-3 (King James Version)

As I would later discover, keeping and caring for a house all by myself would become important training.

In the aftermath of my divorce, I kept a low profile, secretly hoping to receive a break from the storms of life. Play small. Play safe. Stay on the predictable, stable, secure, expected path. No surprises. I ordered my life by a calendar, a clock, and a schedule, both personally and professionally. Spontaneity and deviations from a well-planned-out sched- ule were discouraged. I was now thinking that the more control I had, the fewer opportunities there would be for a storm to pop up. I would attempt to micromanage even the smallest of details to exert that control.

Nowhere did I look more to exert that control than in my job as a hospital pharmacist. Even though my initial career inclination was to study sports medicine, a reaction to medication during high school redirected my path to pursue a pharmacy degree instead. That career turned out to be well suited to a triple Virgo who shines in the details. As analytical problem solvers, Virgos are clear thinkers in the midst of chaos. They love to serve, and they're hardworking, practical, rational, meticulous organizers, and big on accountability.

Throughout my hospital pharmacy career, I enjoyed the challenge of taking on new projects despite my initial doubts that "certainly there are people more qualified than I am to take this on." Then I was reminded that God doesn't call the qualified, He qualifies the called. I was promoted to inpatient oncology pharmacist and developed the pharmacy service portion for our new oncology and stem cell transplant unit. Later I was called upon to redesign our outpatient infusion pharmacy service line to better serve the patients, nurses, and our pharmacy department. The changes would help us create a delivery of care that was safer and more efficient.

As an oncology pharmacist, I loved designing precisely timed chemotherapy administration schedules. Orchestrating a myriad of variables was like conducting a symphony of certainty. It was a way of creating order and predictability for me, for my oncology nurses, and mostly for the patients, who relinquish so much control in their lives to a diagnosis of cancer. However, together we learned that the more conditions and details you try to control, the more control eludes you. A better approach is to invest in planning but be prepared to pivot and adjust. There are appropriate times to want (and be) an unmoving, dependable guide and point of reference. Yet other times may call for remaining flexible and adaptable in the face of changing conditions where course corrections are called for.

Ten more years of being both a divorced mom and hospital pharmacist passed quickly. In 2015, a storm that had been looming on the horizon arrived. It wasn't a sudden and violent storm; rather it was a rite of passage that I had known would arrive one day. My son, now a man, moved to his first apartment, leaving me as an empty nester. After my divorce, I was no longer a wife. When your child leaves the nest, what does motherhood look like? Who was I now?

I wanted a life of more than just being identified by my job title. I had provided my son roots and wings, but what kind of shape were my wings in? Now I was really alone. Living safe and small had served me in the past. It had gotten me here, but it wasn't really living—it was more like existing. It was time to chart a new path for my life.

The Lord says, "I will guide you along
the best pathway for your life.
I will advise you and watch over you."

Psalm 32:8 (NLT)

New doors of opportunity to volunteer opened for me. I volunteered with Samaritan's Purse in Vilonia, Arkansas, to help build new homes in a community leveled by a tornado a year earlier. I also embarked on the adventure of becoming a volunteer assistant lighthouse keeper on St. Helena Island in northern Lake Michigan. This opportunity would change the course of my life.

A willingness to serve and a newfound curiosity about lighthouses compelled me to research and study them more in depth, introducing me to a new word, *pharology*. Inexplicably, I had been traveling to this area in northern Michigan for twenty-five years, passing lighthouses along the way that I didn't really take notice of or know anything about. Now all I could see were the multitude of lighthouses!

I learned of the efforts to restore lighthouses previously owned by the government but offloaded in government auctions to community groups or private individuals interested in preserving these historic structures. The responsibility remained with the US Coast Guard to keep the light shining and fog whistle operational, but these otherwise abandoned structures were deteriorating because of age, neglect, weather, and sometimes vandalism.

So, what kind of person volunteers for a job keeping an offshore lighthouse? Perhaps someone who has lost her way and is looking for guidance in resurrecting, redeeming, and restoring her own life and purpose. After all, a lighthouse stands to guide the journey of the traveler.

> What lies beneath White Shoal Lighthouse remains a mystery to most. The lighthouse is positioned on a rocky shoal—a hidden hazard to ships. She stands as a warning but also a welcoming guide encouraging mariners on their way. Also hidden below the water is the wooden crib that supports the tower. The crib is filled with millions of pounds of stone and concrete as the light's foundation. The lighthouse stands strong because of what you can't see and don't know is there.

I spent three summers volunteering at St. Helena Island before exploring a new opportunity at an offshore lighthouse even more remote and isolated in the waters of northern Lake Michigan and in need of extensive restoration work. When the White Shoal Light restoration project was announced in May 2018, I reached out immediately and asked how I could help. Previously, I had seen only the exterior of the lighthouse while looking up from a tour boat on the water, but I would get the opportunity to explore the inside of the structure in October 2018 to see just how serious I was about helping.

> When first constructed, White Shoal Lighthouse was ornately adorned with Grecian columns and pediments, glazed and glistening white terra cotta tiles, and a silver lantern room roof. Imagine having such a grand look in the middle of northern Lake Michigan! No one traveling by water would ever see her up close

to appreciate this detail. She was built to be viewed from a distance.

Four of us, along with a co-owner of the lighthouse, chartered a boat from Mackinac Island and waited for a weather window to open up to make the twenty-five-mile voyage out to tour White Shoal that fall. Traveling to and from the lighthouse is like that. We choose a date and time of departure and see if Mother Nature gives us her blessing.

This was the first of many challenges I would face while charting a new path for my life. My tests on this trip included handling the round-trip boat ride, climbing the twenty-two-foot ladder between the boat and the lighthouse and all the stairs leading up to the lantern room, and being comfortable with the isolation and remoteness of the location.

A bigger question loomed, however. What would be my reaction to and assessment of the restoration work ahead? This closer look at the structure revealed an aging, fading, and deteriorating exterior caused by neglect, weather, wildlife (cormorants), and water. Cracking and crumbling exterior concrete and interior plaster. Peeling interior paint. It was also clear that the outside was getting inside. . . . We observed water, dead birds, and spiders. Water is both a friend and a foe out here.

> It turns out the original terra cotta tiles weren't a good fit for Lake Michigan weather. The tiles started cracking in the seasonal freeze-thaw cycle. Eventually the beautiful white tiles

were coated with a black tarry substance as a stopgap measure for ten years before the entire tower was entombed with concrete. The ornate architecture was now buried and hidden from view. In 1954, White Shoal would receive its now familiar red-and-white candy-cane-stripe daymark.

The inside of the tower had been gutted when the light was automated and emptied of personnel back in 1976. The first need was to make the structure habitable again. This would be no small feat. Restoring plumbing, re-creating an off-grid electrical supply, and establishing a kitchen, bathroom, and bedrooms would all be required for volunteers to live and work out here.

Count me in! The light that had been inwardly dimmed was now shining a little brighter and outwardly, excited by this opportunity. I could see myself here. As an introvert, I would have no problems working in this remote location with a small crew of volunteers. In fact, I would relish it! The boat rides, the ladder climb to and from the boat, the 159 steps inside the tower, the work to be done—I would gladly accept those challenges and more.

We had a calm boat ride to and from the light that inspection day in 2018. It was a bit naive of me to think that all our boat rides would be like that. They would not.

Once again, the voice of doubt spoke up. "You wear the hat of a hospital pharmacist. Just what is it that you bring to the table here that will be of any practical use?" As it turns out, the attributes and skills that served me as a pharmacist could also be put to use on this project. Years of assessing medication inventory needs for inpatient chemotherapy admissions and daily outpatient infusion appointments would assist me in planning for food and other supplies needed and tracking inventory on hand at the lighthouse. Managing patient schedules would help me manage the complexity and nuances of volunteer schedules at an offshore station.

Looking out for the safety of hospital patients would turn my eye to the safety needs out at the lighthouse. Because of our remote location, responses to urgent or emergent medical situations needed to be assessed and an incident action plan developed with our county emergency medical services director. I would also stock an over-the-counter kit of meds, multiple first aid kits, and two automated external defibrillators on station to support those urgent or emergent needs. That was just the beginning.

What I learned about adhering to firm and inflexible schedules as a pharmacist would apply here as well. Adaptability and flexibility would be much more useful traits to possess in this environment. When changes in weather alter planned departures to and from the lighthouse, I adjust, even when those changes leave me all alone at the lighthouse overnight. Being surrounded by water is a constant reminder to "go with the flow."

In 2020, I listened to a still, small voice confirming a new calling on my life and decided to retire from my thirty-two-year career in pharmacy. Undaunted by the unfolding pandemic, I sold my home and moved from Wisconsin to Michigan to take on the volunteer role of head lighthouse keeper for White Shoal Light. I traded pharmacy for pharology and the opportunity of keeping a much bigger house. This would now be my year-round work both onshore and offshore, and in this role I discovered that divinity, rather than drudgery, can be found in the many duties of lighthouse keeping.

This journey to help restore a lighthouse really was a journey to restore myself. I would find my voice again and use it in a new way, telling the stories of the light's history on our Facebook page, in museum exhibits, and in lighthouse publications. The lighthouse has more than a century of stories to be discovered and told, and I have a shared purpose here as well to unearth and give voice to my own. I didn't foresee this path for my life, but storms came and cleared the way!

> My first storm while out at the lighthouse was a windstorm. No thunder. No lightning. No rain. A sound like a speeding, shaking freight train within the tower woke us up after midnight. We just had to take a look outside for ourselves, not knowing what we would see or experience in the dark.

The 2022 season ended much the same way it started. This time a change in wind speed and direction arrived much earlier than originally forecast, and our team didn't have the ability to wait it out or try again the next day. Unable to re-moor the boat, we were committed to traveling back to the mainland. We had to quickly finish the loading process and get untied from the concrete crib or risk severe damage to our only means of transportation. The three of us were in no-man's-land in the middle of northern Lake Michigan. Our heading would be directly into the twenty-five-knot east winds. Six-foot waves would pound the boat the entire twenty-two-mile journey back to the marina in Mackinaw City. Despite being bounced and beaten up by the unrelenting waves, we arrived back safely. Did I mention soaking wet? Everyone and everything on board was soaking wet. Next season I'm investing in waterproof rather than water-resistant gear. Details are important.

As I write this, I am six months away from turning sixty, and my life remains a work in progress. And the lighthouse? She remains a work in progress as well. She has endured a lot. She is built of strong stuff. She stands in the storms and shines her light.

> A lighthouse keeps watch in the middle of
> northern Lake Michigan.
> Empty. Isolated. Abandoned. Neglected.
> Yet she stands.
> Weathering. Waning. Aging. Fading.
> The outside getting inside.
> Yet still she stands.
> Stalwart. Dependable. Resilient. Guiding.
> Warning. Welcoming. Encouraging.
> She stands in her purpose.
> Built to be seen and sometimes heard.

Yielding to restoration.
What is contained inside and what lies beneath
are hidden and remain unknown to most.
The lighthouse and I are one.
The lighthouse is me.
I stand in the storms and shine my light.

ABOUT THE AUTHOR

JILL
ORE

A divorce, an empty nest, and retirement from a 32-year hospital pharmacy career had Jill Ore wondering what came next. During an unfolding pandemic, she left her home state of Wisconsin to become head lighthouse keeper at White Shoal Lighthouse located offshore in northern Lake Michigan. Tending the lighthouse taught her to tend the light within. She discovered that it was possible to restore meaning and purpose in her own life, despite the storms that had blown her off course. Learn more about the lighthouse at preservewhiteshoal.org

Chapter 10

FIND YOURSELF

Amey Stark-Foust

"I am responsible for
my own happiness."

I spent most of my life searching for love and happiness in all the wrong places. I traveled through hell and took a few detours, all in the name of trying to figure out who I was and what made me happy. I floundered in a sea of mistakes while searching for my identity. The extent of my self-doubt and insecurity was simply not healthy. Throughout life's journey, in a variety of circumstances, the trials I encountered left me with deep wounds that I wasn't sure how to heal. Those excruciating soul wounds left me starving for attention and affection, and although I may not have realized it at the time, my mental health suffered greatly. But even with all my flaws, God removed me from a dark place and set me on a healing journey that allowed me to find myself and my true source of happiness.

Two separate times during my teenage years, I was the victim of sexual abuse. I was reluctant to identify myself as a victim, but many more emotions manifested themselves in how I felt about men and how I treated myself. When you have not been respected from the beginning, by the first male figure in your life, you seek affirmation from men at all costs.

When I began dating at age fifteen, my expectations for how a woman should be treated were very low. I was happy to get any male attention, whether it came with honorable intentions or not, and most of the time it did not. The cost for me was my self-esteem, dignity, and self-respect. It created a mentality in me that any love I received needed to be earned instead of freely given. I had no idea what my worth was, and I continually looked to outside sources to provide validation. Compounded by feelings of guilt and shame, I found myself longing for something I had never really had, real love from someone of the opposite sex.

I've come to realize that self-worth comes early in a young woman's life as she develops a relationship with her father. Lots of positive affirmations lay the foundation for all her future relationships with men. Whatever a father gives or doesn't give his daughter affects her expectations of all men who enter her life in the future. My father was present only for the first few years of my life. Once my parents were divorced, years went by when I didn't see him at all. Many of those years I didn't receive a birthday or Christmas gift, and I recall only a handful of phone calls to check on me. By the time I was eight years old, he had faded into the background of my life, and my mom and I had moved from a small town in Texas (Hamilton) to the big city (Houston), five hours away. On multiple occasions, my mother had my father arrested when he stopped paying child support. He did not attend my high school graduation or walk me down the aisle when I was married.

I met a young man at work, working in the same department of a French-owned hypermarket similar to a Walmart. I remember how enamored I was with the idea that he had a "bad boy" flair. He was a loss prevention investigator, arresting shoplifters and the like, but something about him intrigued me. Our courtship was very short, and after a few months we both thought we were in love. It wasn't long before we were married.

At the age of nineteen I had absolutely no idea who I was or what true love really was. With each passing year, we both made many mistakes. Neither of us had solid fatherly examples, and we both carried a great deal of baggage and feelings into our marriage. I was still searching for my identity and for the type of love I saw on television and in movies, and in the relationships of a few family members and friends' parents. I was keenly aware that no one had a perfect life, but I was certain that the example I'd had as a child was not the type of relationship I wanted for myself. Life and my marriage became frustrating, and I felt as if I was in a relationship very similar to my childhood relationship with my father, lacking affirmation and respect. I longed to know what those things felt like, and I was certain no male in my life had ever had those kinds of feelings for me.

I became a mom at age twenty and quickly absorbed a new identity as someone's mother. You put all your own needs in a lockbox and toss the key for the next eighteen years.

Whatever insecurities I had were suddenly put on hold as I proudly took on the role of mom. With the birth of my second child four years later, I became mom to two people, further cementing my role while putting the rest of my identity on hold. Being a mom to my children held the absolute highest honor in my book, and I was ever so proud to set aside my own personal needs to fulfill that very important role.

When my children were young, I often relished the idea of a solo trip to the grocery store just for a quiet moment to myself. As they grew older and became involved in their respective activities, I simply lost myself in what they were doing, living vicariously through both of them. I wanted to make certain that I didn't repeat my childhood, where I looked around a crowded room and realized that all the other children had someone there to support them and I did not. I was determined that they would never know what that felt like.

As my children grew, I took great pride and pleasure in attending every event they participated in, and I would not trade that part of my life for any amount of money. I was a team mom for both of their sports, and I spent many years serving on booster club boards in different capacities. I tried to stay as busy as I could while suppressing the feelings and insecurities that plagued me on the inside. I was using all the busyness to keep my mind off other things that were weighing heavily upon me. Some of my friends joked that I had a superhero cape because I did it all. Aside from finding my identity, I was seeking the affirmation I so desperately desired. In my search for internal fulfillment, no other role that I took on provided that.

After the first eleven tumultuous years of marriage, accompanied by the excitement and joy of raising our beautiful children, my husband and I tried to start fresh by renewing our wedding vows. This was the perfect opportunity to hit the reset button.

But no amount of throwing myself into my marriage, showing my love and appreciation for my husband while sharing in the joys of raising our children, got me any closer to finding my self-worth. Nor did it get me closer to finding the true source of happiness that my heart longed for. In fact, I sank deeper and deeper into withdrawal, and some days I felt as if I were simply going through the motions of life. From the outside looking in, I had the perfect family, a great job, beautiful children, a nice home, and so on. But on the inside, I was struggling with my issues. I feared the tensions in our home would teach my children the negative aspects of a relationship, and I tried to be as strong as possible for their sake.

As they grew and became more independent, they needed me less and less, which only created gaps of time where I was forced to participate in life with my husband more often. Since I didn't know who I was outside of being a mom, I didn't even know how to enjoy my free time. I had spent many years devoting every ounce of energy and time to raising and being there for my children. To this day, I would not change that part of my life, but the reality is, there was little time or energy left for myself.

We spent a few years as the kids were a little older going kayaking with friends at the lake, and took some wonderful, relaxing vacations. Those moments felt like opportunities to find things that interested us as a couple so we could live out the last half of our lives enjoying each other. Days turned into weeks, months, and eventually years. Our children were both out of high school, and although there were moments of absolute bliss, I knew something was missing, and I withdrew even more. Friends asked us to go out and do things, but I often had to go by myself, which made me feel very sad and alone. My husband had already begun to do the things that made him happy, and they didn't include me. I wanted the camaraderie of being around people, but I also longed to share those moments with the person I felt God had blessed me with.

Off and on throughout my marriage, I was involved in church at various levels, but after moving to Dallas I allowed my children's activities to take precedence. During this time, I was not getting spiritually fed, and I believe that showed in many ways. Both of my children had been baptized early in their lives and I was quite certain they knew right from wrong, but I knew that my lack of a relationship with God was preventing me from being the parent they deserved to see. When things worsened, I cried out to God for help with my marriage, like we all tend to do when we're in crisis mode.

That was the beginning of my reconnection, and His comfort carried me through several years where things became so depressing that some days I could hardly breathe. At those times, I was convinced that if our family had been more involved in a church community, things would not have fallen apart the way they did. Maybe we would have spent more time together discovering and growing as a couple rather than developing separate lives and growing further apart. Now that my healing journey has begun, I know that God removed me from my situation and is preparing me for something beyond my wildest dreams.

Early in 2020, after separating from my husband, I moved downtown to an apartment close to my office. It quickly became my personal sanctuary, and I focused more on healing. The move coincided with the pandemic and lockdown, and I spent many days working from home and taking advantage of lunch breaks to walk the trails. There was amazing scenery, and I listened to a variety of music stations, depending on my mood. Some days I needed to hear praise music to be reminded of who was in control and how fortunate I was to have this time to walk and clear my head. Other days I found myself listening to eighties rock music while stepping to the beat or singing along. I got a few strange looks while on the trails, but I was becoming more confident in myself and wasn't bothered by the stares.

Not surprisingly, my marriage had suffered from my unhappiness and my husband's neglect, so we filed for divorce, and after ninety days it was final. I spent several days and nights in shock that after twenty-nine years of marriage, it was gone in the blink of an eye. I wasn't sure what came next, but I knew I had to keep moving forward. Some days it felt like one step forward and two steps back, and other days it felt like I had made great progress.

Eventually I set out on a new adventure and began dating. Going on a date for the first time since I had met my husband at nineteen years of age, I was a ball of nerves yet still excited at the idea. Dating online was a very different and often scary process: people would misrepresent themselves, have hidden agendas, and were often downright dishonest. They would expect to meet someone who fulfilled their ideas of a perfect mate, yet they were not being truthful to the prospects they met.

The very first exclusive relationship after my long marriage proved to be a short season, but one that helped me begin to heal from some of my past wounds. Instinctively, I somehow knew this was not my forever relationship, but he brought me out of my shell, taught me the benefits of truly forgiving someone, and set me on a path in the right direction. I began to learn how to let go, how to use the opportunities in front of me to try new things and stretch my boundaries. The first thing that sticks in my mind so vividly, with my fear of heights, was parasailing on the beach in Florida—allowing myself to fully trust and let go as I went up into the air . . . far higher than I would normally be comfortable with. I released my fear, and it allowed me to feel the wind and glide ever so smoothly, high above the ocean. It was peaceful and I felt free.

On a warm, sunny day, while the sunlight came through the trees, I sat in the front yard of my apartment enjoying a glass of wine. I remember going over the pros and cons of renting versus owning my own home. I met my real estate agent that day, and through his gentle persuasion, I was convinced that being a homeowner would be in my best interest. Never mind that we were in the middle of a pandemic; we looked at about 185 homes over the course of a few months (both online and in person). I had gone from that scared, shy woman of almost fifty to a woman ready to take charge of her new life and dive headfirst into the next adventure. That adventure led me to the purchase of my very own home! I could not contain my enthusiasm. I knew that my faithfulness to God had manifested itself in homeownership, and, remarkably, a purchase where there was a connection between the sellers and my boss. What are the odds that I would look at so many homes over the course of a few months and ultimately purchase one from someone whose boss was a dear friend of my boss for forty years? This most assuredly confirmed my faith yet again.

Later, I learned that my real estate agent's wife was a talented photographer with an eye for helping women look and feel like movie stars. I had always wanted to do a special type of photo shoot, probably for different reasons back then, but this time to continue building my long-lost self-esteem. Our session was once called a "boudoir shoot," which sounds provocative, but my time with her, along with her expertise and elegant approach, made me feel like I was discovering the woman I yearned to be and helped me embark on a journey to change the feelings I had about myself while continuing to search for who I was after so many life changes.

When the proofs arrived, I could not believe I was looking at myself. I even asked the photographer, "Are you sure that's me?" My session was ultimately one of the forty-women-over-forty photo shoots that the photographer would complete. I can only imagine that the other thirty-nine women in this project felt the same level of confidence I received from my session. I began to see myself in a completely different light. Still uncertain if the woman in the photos was me, I thought, *Wow, this woman is beautiful and was made by God, for His purpose.* It wasn't just about gaining self-esteem; it was also the realization that I no longer needed anyone else's validation. The session made me feel empowered and confident, not just in myself, but in my ability to handle work and personal challenges, taking them all in stride. God knew me with all my faults and flaws; He had protected me through many of life's trials and was allowing me to see myself as He saw me, broken but beautiful.

As I basked in the assurance of who I was becoming, I knew there was still work to be done. My relationship with the first man I dated after my divorce had ended, and I knew if I wanted to try dating again, I had to "get back up on the horse." I had to muster up all my newfound confidence to try to discover if indeed there was someone out there for me. During this time, people gave me a great deal of advice, as they often do. "You're rushing things. Why are you dating?" or "Do you think it's too soon?" or "You need this type of person or that type of person, with this type of job or that type of job." "You need to find or date someone of this stature or who has this much money in the bank."

Although I always appreciated the fact that the people closest to me cared for my safety and well-being, I knew I had to take all advice (good, bad, or indifferent) with a grain of salt. This was my time now, to shine my light brighter than ever before. To live the life I had always dreamed possible and to meet that special someone to share things with until the end of time. I relied on my own instincts and felt comfortable in my own skin. That does not mean my instincts were always spot-on, but it does mean I tried to use my heart as a guide when meeting people.

In His timing, God will bring the man I have longed for into my life. Until that time comes, and although I sometimes find it difficult to comprehend, He will provide the love and adoration that I have desperately missed. He cherishes us and has since before we were conceived. The mere thought of us was His idea, and His love and adoration are enough.

> *"For You created my innermost parts;*
> *You wove me in my mother's womb."*

Psalm 139:13 (NASB)

In the process of living and writing this small but very significant chapter of my life, I have met a few extraordinary people who have encouraged me to be my authentic self, to learn to say no when I need to, and to understand that

I am responsible for my own happiness. Although I am far from mastering it, I am learning how to also set boundaries in all aspects of my life. This new mindset goes against the very grain of not only who I am on the inside, but who I was for many years through learned behavior. I was such a people pleaser that I would often heed the advice of family and friends to the detriment of my own happiness. Everyone's needs came before my own, and their happiness seemed dependent on me and what I did or didn't do for them. I second-guessed myself a lot and put my wants and desires on the back burner while making sure those around me succeeded, thrived, and were content. What I realized later was that during that time I had lost myself and my identity in pleasing others.

What I thought represented love most assuredly did not. Being lonely and without an identity, self-esteem, or an understanding of my own self-worth often made daily life feel heavy. I am so incredibly grateful that I have been able to lean on the Lord to fulfill that fatherly role that I so deeply missed. It took some time before I surrendered to His will and purpose for my life. I spent many years attempting to handle problems on my own and discovering that the only way to have complete peace about any situation is to trust in God's plan for us.

I still make mistakes, even though I know the things I should choose. I still struggle with making and keeping boundaries in place. I still find dating over fifty, after a twenty-nine-year marriage, to be the most complex thing to navigate in today's world under the scrutiny of family, friends, and prospective mates. I still believe beyond a shadow of a doubt that there is a perfect life partner for me. Not perfect in who he is, but perfect for me. Created just for me and designed (maybe even hardwired) to fulfill all the desires of my heart, both emotionally and physically. Each day I find myself closer to understanding who I am, what I want, and what the next steps are to moving forward.

Through the storms and trials of life, I have finally found my identity. I know God has a purpose for me, and each day I try to live in a way that makes Him proud. He loves me uncon-ditionally, even with all my flaws. He protected me from myself and from things I didn't even realize. He heard things I couldn't hear and made the moves I wouldn't make. Whether life is healthy or toxic, we get complacent and comfortable in what we know. Making changes can often be very scary, but most of the time they're very necessary. Every day I have something to be thankful for, and today I am thankful for His grace that saved me and set me free.

ABOUT THE AUTHOR

AMEY
STARK-FOUST

Amey Stark-Foust has spent her life trying to understand herself. As a wife and mother, she put all other wants and needs on the back burner. It wasn't until she was separated and ultimately divorced that she realized something was missing from her life. A journey of self-reflection helped her discover herself and the vivacious, spirited woman who had been hiding for years. She named her crafting business Resilient, after receiving a bracelet with that word on it from a close family member. Now Amey uses the faith and strength she gained through hardships to help other women see themselves as their creator does. To learn more about Amey's journey and how she has found her identity, visit @resilient.tx on Instagram or @resilienttx on Facebook.

Chapter 11

REWRITE YOUR STORIES

Cami Foerster

"Stories that are repeated become truths we believe."

"I have never seen you this stressed."

Those words from my primary health care provider shook me to my core. "I don't believe anything I can give you will help." He had never said that to me before, not once in the seven years I'd been seeing him. Not when I was living amidst the stress of losing my job and relocating my entire family from New England to the Rocky Mountains. Not when I homeschooled one of my kids through middle school while pursuing my master's degree. Not when my family was surviving an intense season of mental health issues. Not when I watched from afar as my hometown burned to the ground in a matter of hours. Not when my family and friends were out of contact as they fled from the flames that threatened to burn them alive. Not when I held my dad's hand as he breathed his last rattled breath. Not when the grief from all I had lost washed over me like a tidal wave.

"I have never seen you this stressed." And he was right. Twelve days later, those words of truth still hung in the air as I had a major panic attack while driving home from a Sabbath day's drive. Gasping for breath, I found myself pulled over on the side of the road; hours from home I hit rock bottom. I had nothing left. Not for me, not for my friends, not for my family. Nothing.

And then I did what I had only fantasized about.

Thousands of times.

I ran away from home.

Running Away

And I ran back home.

When I was a little kid and felt overwhelmed and scared, I would pull the covers over my head. I blocked out all the triggers and hid until the overwhelming feelings went away. That instinct kicked in immediately, and I just wanted to go home. Not to the home I had created as an adult, but the home I grew up in as a little kid. The home where I could pull a blanket over my head and shut out the world until the panic stopped.

Within twenty-four hours, I cleared my calendar, packed up my truck, and followed my instinct.

I left the Rocky Mountains for the Sierra Foothills.

Honestly, I don't remember much of the drive. Yes, I drove. It is a 1200-mile trip that requires at least nineteen hours of driving time, not including stops. It's a familiar drive for me. I have lost count of how many times I have watched the land change through my windshield. Driving gifts me with space and solitude. Space to let the day progress at my own pace. Solitude to hear myself think. Space to feel the emotions that have forced their way to the top of my being. Solitude to find the freedom that allows the emotions to roll through my body.

What I do remember is the feeling of simultaneously running away from my current life and running toward my past. I was running away from a life in which I felt trapped. That was the life I had built for myself. It was a life that had space for everyone but me. While driving I passed through the desert that lay between the mountains of my current life and the mountains of my childhood—both literally and symbolically. The desert landscape has pathways, rocks, small towns, boulders, and dilapidated buildings. It echoes a life that was once thriving but has become obsolete and increasingly devoid of color, and has fallen into desolation from neglect.

But I was also running toward the safety and joy I had known in my past. Although the structures of my childhood home had been destroyed by fire (a reality that was not lost on me), my instinct was to return home. I needed connection at the most basic level, and I was drawn back to the land that supported me as I grew from a freckle-nosed kid into a naïve teenager ready to take on the world. I was running toward the freedom and love I knew as a child—to be in the space where my story started.

Arriving Home

The end of my long drive brought me to the concrete foundation of what was once my dad's garage. Thanks to a couple of childhood friends, I had dinner and a tent and I was seen. Here I was, feeling like a broken and desperate mess, and these two friends met me where I was without judgment and supported me with food and shelter. They welcomed me home.

The next day, I walked the land. It was very different, having been completely devastated and transformed by the fire three years earlier, but as I walked through the dust and the brush, I remembered the good. I remembered feeling warm and safe in front of the giant fireplace that sat in the corner of our living room. I remembered family meals gathered around the table with the smell of steak and steamed broccoli coming from the kitchen. I remembered walking down the hallway to my parents' bedroom to surprise my dad on his birthday with an impromptu visit. I remembered teaching my niece to bake by first dusting our faces with flour. I remembered watching the different critters that would pass through our backyard: deer, raccoons, owls, and turkeys. Even though the buildings were gone, the land remembered the good. And I remembered it too. I was home.

Returning to the Start of My Story

On the land is the shell of an old oak tree that once stood by my dad's garage. The outside was now white, and a large crack down the front exposed a hollow, blackened core.

Standing at a fraction of its original height, this tree captured my attention with its haunting beauty. It was a signpost to me, reminding me that I had a choice. When challenges and tragedy came into my life, would they destroy me, or would they shape me? The fire had destroyed the land, including this tree. But three years later, the land was beginning to recover with new growth and new life. Likewise, the challenges and tragedies I had endured over the previous seven years had reduced me to a shell of myself. Could I recover? That would depend on what I chose to hold on to as I moved forward and what I chose to prune.

Honest reflection is terrifying. But the stories we remember and the stories we tell ourselves come from somewhere—a comment, a feeling, a perspective, an experience. Stories that are repeated become truths we believe. These beliefs then inform our actions. My actions led me to a panic attack in the Rocky Mountains. My path toward restoration demanded that I examine what I believed and where those beliefs came from. I needed the courage to explore the half-lies that had stunted my growth and excavate the nugget of truth. Through patience, compassion, and curiosity I became honest with myself about what I believed, what was true, and what was false.

Half-Lie #1: Stay Quiet

As a little girl, I was painfully shy. In fact, I would make my younger sister order for me when we went to a restaurant. I felt shame and embarrassment in speaking up for myself. There are a million potential reasons for that, but I remember wanting to stay out of the limelight. Ironically, I had spent time on stage, dancing and singing, from the age of four. This dual experience created a dichotomy in me. I knew how to perform "on stage" or in public, and I kept how I truly felt "off stage" or in private.

I also clearly remember learning that if I had an opinion, I should keep it to myself. It started as protective wisdom from my dad. He was a private man, and he knew that most people like to hear themselves talk. He also knew that many people hold their own opinion as more valuable than anyone else's. In hindsight, I realized he was trying to teach me how to protect myself from being rejected or ridiculed. However, my childhood self learned instead that I should stay quiet. Instead of hearing it was okay for me to have an opinion, I believed I was better off having no opinion at all.

As I got older, this half-lie took hold in a big way. I hated arguing with people and would discount my own opinion before someone else had a chance to tear it down. I deferred to anyone with authority over me or in leadership positions, even when my spirit knew I was right. In family matters, with so many differing opinions, it was easier for me not to have one. In fact, on a recent trip to Disney World, I was asked what I wanted to do that day and my mind was a complete blank. I had no opinion to voice.

Half-Lie #2: Be Helpful

As the oldest of three kids, I grew up as "Mommy's little helper." Eager to please and glowing when I received a compliment, I found that helping came naturally to me. Although I don't ever remember being told that it was my job to make others happy, I grew up believing that was true. I wanted to make my mom happy by being a good girl, and I wanted to make my dad happy by being smart in school. Top marks in school brought rewards and praise. Making someone else happy gave me good feelings. I guess no one was surprised when I was awarded the superlative of Most Helpful in high school.

It made me feel good. It was reinforced when I became more serious about my Christian faith. As I was becoming a young adult, I learned an acronym designed to help us balance our priorities and lead to J.O.Y.—Jesus first, Others next, Yourself last. That was how to be a good Christian, and I was hardwired to want to be good and make others proud. I took it to heart as a mantra of sorts.

As I grew in my faith, I claimed as my life verse Philippians 2:3-4, which reads, "Do nothing out of selfish ambition or vain conceit. Rather, in humility value others above yourselves, not looking to your own interests but each of you to the interests of the others" (New International Version). Couple that verse with Colossians 3:23, which says, "Whatever you do, work heartily, as for the Lord and not for men" (English Standard Version), and I created a belief and held to it wholeheartedly. I was to serve and help others as an act of service to God. My needs came last.

My innate helpful nature latched on to this new belief and amplified it into an unbalanced and unhealthy directive.

Internally, my self-esteem became locked together with serving others. I saw my only value as being a servant to others, downplaying my own unique talents and gifts, and hinging my happiness on others' approval. As I developed a silent martyr's identity, work and service became my God, and it robbed me of all joy.

Half-Lie #3: Perfection Is a Virtue

I was a smart kid. School came naturally, and I rarely had to work at it. Praise and affirmation was my fuel, which spurred me on to continue to achieve. I excelled in multiple subjects and continuously found myself at the top of my class. In one sense, it appeared as if I were thriving. Who wouldn't be thriving when they were achieving so much success? Right?

However, our family lived by the saying "Anything worth doing is worth doing well." My experience was teaching me that doing something well was the same as doing something perfectly. I was perfect in school, and that was seen as me doing my best. So "doing well" and "doing my best" melded together to mean "doing perfectly."

As time went on, I became a perfectionist. I graduated as valedictorian of my high school class. The first B I earned was in college, and it devastated me. I kept pushing myself to be the best in every area—my education, my marriage, and my career. When I fell short of perfection in any area, I would beat myself up internally. My flaws and failures were clearer than my successes and achievements. The more I strived to live up to the impossible standard of perfection, the more I believed I was a failure.

Half-Lie #4: I Am Broken

As a teenager, I wondered what was wrong with me. I saw myself as overly emotional, feeling everything in a deep way. Emotions were a roller coaster, and I truly loved the highs and valued the lows. But then I learned that my emotions were untrustworthy, excessive, and something to be managed or hidden. I learned that if my emotions got too big, I should go away somewhere private and return only when I could make better sense. Living in a world and a family where intelligence and rationality were highly valued, I began to equate being emotional with being broken.

I specifically remember feeling very sad and arguing with myself that I had no reason to feel that way. I was in a family that loved me, I had friends at school, and I found success in just about everything I did. But I felt empty. I was doing everything right—perfectionism pushed me to excellence, being Most Helpful as a people pleaser meant I was well liked, and I kept my voice quiet to keep the peace and not rock the boat. I was blessed, but I felt alone and broken. Rationally, I had no right to feel that way, but my heart told me otherwise.

Growing up when mental health issues were minimized and something to be ashamed of, I believed I was fundamentally flawed. I had value as long as I could perform up to others' expectations, but it was best to keep my true self hidden. I suffered with chronic depression, and to survive the suicidal thoughts and relentless stream of negative self-talk, I divided myself. "On stage" I presented my public face that most people knew and liked. "Off stage" my private self wrestled with her demons and made sure they stayed hidden so I could be rational and sensible when I stepped back on stage. Through the years, depression has been an unwelcomed acquaintance who continues to follow me.

Thankfully, there have been seasons of respite amidst my travels through what I now call the Valley of Defeat. I'm grateful when I can feel joy, warmth, and love because I know it is a gift that is not guaranteed to me. Because eventually, when the depressive feelings return, I am again tempted to believe that I am a fatally broken person.

Each of those half-lies I believed were exactly that. They were partial lies with a nugget of truth. They were out of balance and exaggerated by other aspects of my life—being partly true and partly false. That was the world according to Cami, and at their genesis those beliefs helped me navigate my world. However, as I continued to grow and mature, the incompleteness of those truths grew to be a form of harmful decay weakening my core. And just like the black, hollow core of the dead oak tree, my now-harmful beliefs were exposed. I needed to heed the warning of the tree and find a way to heal what was decaying in my soul. It was time to quit hiding from myself and let go of the half-lies and beliefs that were destroying me. It was time to turn toward full truths and foster my healing from the inside out.

Returning home to California brought me into an intense journey of emotions, thoughts, and experiences. Fortunately I was held by a group of friends from my growing-up years who kept me safe and fed as I searched for my way forward and inward. They advised sleep, alerting me to the reality that I had not slept well for years. I had to relearn how to sleep! They prompted me to journal out my thoughts and emotions, both to let out the parts that were harmful to me and to record the process of discovery. They reminded me of what was good, nurturing me with the blessings of gratitude. They allowed me to be broken and loved me freely. They held needed space for me to heal. And thus began my Selah Journey.

My Selah Journey

In five weeks' time, I was able to drive home without feeling panicked. I have continued the practices I clung to as lifelines that allowed me to take a good, honest look at who I was and allow healing into the broken places. My Selah Journey didn't change my circumstances, but it did change me. In this journey of a lifetime I have found peace with myself and a process to guide me through life's challenges. Although I know there is much in my life that I don't have any control over, I do have a responsibility to myself, my family, and others to be fully me within this life. I am free from the half-lies that kept me in a weakened state. I am becoming more whole every day because I live out The Selah Journey. It is a great privilege to share it with you.

#IChooseMe

My very first step was to allow myself to be just as important as everyone else in my life. I didn't realize I was doing that when I ran away, but that is exactly what I did. In clearing my calendar of what other people wanted from me or had planned for me, I was able to give myself a schedule that met my needs for time, space, connection, and rhythm. Did I disappoint some folks? Yes. Did they understand what I was doing? No. But I had deprioritized myself so significantly that my physical body had to bring me to my knees and demand that I stop. I needed to make a new decision.

I chose to allow myself to be just as important as the person I sit next to. If I would advise someone else to rest when tired, I could extend that same wisdom to myself. If I could remind a friend that their emotions matter, I could allow that same truth to be true for me. Before my Selah Journey, I knew self-care was important. However, my people-pleasing self still insisted that it come after taking care of others first. By flipping the script on myself, I acknowledged that I deserved the same loving-kindness from myself that I extended to others with ease. My selfcare is my responsibility, and it starts when I Choose Me.

#SabbathResting

I was first introduced to the concept of Sabbath in my college days. It is found in some religious systems in which a full day every week is set aside for rest and worship. I was intrigued by the idea and practiced it occasionally but allowed it to fall by the wayside when times were busy. When I arrived in California and my friends confronted me with how exhausted I had become, my eyes were opened to just how vital rest and sleep really are. Before I returned to my Colorado home, I scheduled an appointment with my doctor to make sure correcting my sleep challenges was my number one priority.

Lack of sleep causes harm to our body, mind, and soul. It negatively impacts every area of our lives. Learning to sleep and creating a Sabbath practice has been one way for me to make sure I'm in a healthy state to engage with everything that comes my way. My Sabbath day is my "get to" day instead of my "have to" day. I get to not set my alarm. I get to do things that bring me joy and refresh my spirit. Amazingly, by keeping a regular Sabbath, my mind now tends to order the week around that day. Sabbath Resting is my anchor, essential to keeping me whole.

#TheGiftOfReflection

I am a haphazard journaler at best, and the thought of writing down my experiences felt overwhelming to me at the start of my Selah Journey. Although I did focus on journaling my experiences, I also practiced reflection in other ways. I worked with my counselor to discover and unpack the beliefs that were hurting me. I discussed thoughts and feelings with friends who were a safe sounding board and reminded me I was not alone. I spent time alone in nature, gleaning wisdom from the forest, the rivers, and the animals. And I learned to meditate, creating practices to notice my thoughts and address them in helpful ways as they surfaced.

The gift of reflection is what allowed me to look honestly at my own life. It insisted that I not blame others for choices I make. Reflection has opened me up to learning more about my emotions, intuition, and identity. I credit my intentional practice of reflection for showing me how to move from a place of reacting to my circumstances into the space where I choose to show up in my life each new day. This practice helped me move through the fears that held me back and into a life of freedom. The Gift of Reflection challenges me to become the most authentic version of myself.

#GratitudeAndPraise

Early on in my journal notes, I wrote about my gratitude for water. It refreshes me and grounds me. I love to swim and float, and throughout my first physical Selah Journey, I spent a lot of my time at the lake or with my feet in a creek. Soon afterward, one of my friends gifted me a gratitude journal, and I launched my practice of Gratitude and Praise.

Many studies explain how the practice of gratitude rewires our brains. It is amazing how quickly my outlook changed for the better as I grew in my consistency of this practice. It has taught me that I can always find what I look for. If I look for ways in which I am broken and damaged (as in my former life), I will find it. If I look for the ways in which I am blessed and whole, I will find it. My daily practice of

Gratitude and Praise has transformed the way I see myself and my world.

#MySelahTribe

None of this transformative journey would have happened had it not been for my friends. My Selah Tribe held sacred space for me when I was at the lowest and most vulnerable place in my life. Food, housing, comfort, companionship, wisdom, and safety were just a few of the gifts they provided for me throughout my journey. I know that my journey would have looked very different had they not been there for me.

In reflection, I believe one factor in my critical stress level was how I isolated myself. I walled away who I was, because I believed I was broken and worthless. I didn't allow anyone to see me, because I was confident they would reject me. Fortunately, I was proved wrong. When depression and shame isolate us, they lead to destruction, one way or another. However, when we find courage to allow ourselves to be seen by trustworthy people, it is a different story. My Selah Tribe consisted of those who saw me, encouraged me, and spoke truth to me. I couldn't do this journey without them, nor would I want to. I am who I am because of my Selah Tribe.

An Invitation into Selah

About a year after I had run away from my life and returned again, I was talking with a friend on the phone. Just before we hung up, she stopped me and said, "I don't know what you are doing these days, but you sound so good!"

With tears in my eyes, I thanked her. I told her, "I've been doing my Selah Journey, and it has made all the difference in the world." Gratitude flooded my heart. My life feels completely different now. I enjoy less self-condemnation and more freedom. I guard my times of rest and find the good in every day. I am seen, in truth, and fully loved by my God, my family, my friends, and myself. The Selah Journey has shown me how to walk into thriving. I'm just getting started, and I'd love to have you join me for your own Selah Journey.

Welcome home.

ABOUT THE AUTHOR

CAMI FOERSTER

Cami Foerster traded her childhood stomping grounds of northern California for the majestic Rocky Mountains of Colorado. The fifty-year journey has been filled with spiritual learning, miles of road-tripping, and countless shared cups of coffee (or whiskey) with friends. Her compulsion to help others has been a blessing and a curse, especially when the joy of helping meets her lack of attention to self-care. Through it all, she found *selah*, the rest, reflection, and gratitude that rescued her when the stress of holding her world together caused her to crumble apart.

Now, she is living her Selah Journey and connecting with other weary souls so they can do the same. You can find her at www.theselahjourney.com or on Facebook and Instagram @theselahjourney, even when she retreats into her beloved mountains with family and friends...and whiskey.

Chapter 12

MORPH INTO A NEW WAY OF LIFE

Rikki (Cindy) Shaw

"Survival is in my own hands."

Driving from the pain center in Houston back to my home in Hamilton, Texas, I had an epiphany: it was time to leave my bad marriage. Numerous times my husband had told me that if I cussed him, I was putting myself in a man's place and deserved a man's whipping. He would wrench my arms behind my back and slap my face while I tried to defend myself. Finally, one day he again came at me, only this time I grabbed Amey and the diaper bag and ran out the back door. I jumped over a picket fence and flagged down the first car I saw to take us to safety. Never again would I be the victim of violence.

We often had other veteran husbands and their wives over to eat and play games. All would go smoothly until my husband made fun of me and a fuss would ensue. Obviously, the gathering would end. Soon afterward, he would demand sex, but after being berated in front of company, I was in no mood for sex. He would then force himself on me. Afterward I would get up and go to the living room and wait for him to fall asleep before crawling back into bed.

Many times the wives and I waited until late evening for our husbands to come home from what we called the Green Frog—the green building near the edge of town that was the VFW hall. The men would stay for hours after work, only to return to their homes half drunk and usually combative. Other nights, I would return late and exhausted from working as a surgical nurse but still had to prepare a meal.

I remember one time I served homemade pizza and a salad. My husband came in and announced loudly that he wanted a *meal*, not a snack. He then proceeded to flip the table, and all the food landed on the floor while Amey screamed with fear in her high chair. I just took Amey and we went to my mom's house.

Another time I went to the army base commissary with a friend and stayed away for hours while my husband watched Amey. Upon my return I discovered that he had taken her to the hospital because she had jumped on her bed and split open her forehead, thus requiring four stitches. Back at home, he had given our three-year-old child beer, and now she was drunk.

Happier times were when Amey and I would bottle-feed baby calves until they were ready for auction. We had an above ground pool, and she had a lot of friends over to play, thus avoiding the chaos inside the house. My stunning yellow chrysanthemums, roses, and huge garden kept me occupied and happy as a lark. I canned and froze an abundance of vegetables.

After the episode where the dinner ended up on the floor, I decided it was time to move to Houston. I gathered everything in the house, and off Amey and I went. Then everything about me changed.

I had traveled to a pain center in Houston once a month for several months after a botched back surgery left me unable to walk for three months. My time away from Hamilton gave me effusive pleasure, and I felt an energy pull toward Houston. Even though I felt the pull, it was not easy to leave my friends and the home we called the Little Ponderosa. But there would be many more opportunities in a big city than in a small town of 2,800. Amey would have more opportunities, and I would be able to perform my ventriloquist act in front of much larger crowds.

I had always dreamed of working in the Houston Medical Center as well as at the charity hospital where over ten thousand babies were born annually. I worked at both of those places as a licensed vocational nurse for years until I reinjured my back. As if that wasn't strenuous enough, I began working for an all-women paint company and later had my own business called Le Feminine Touch Paint Company. Now I just perform my ventriloquist act for senior centers and private parties.

I spent a big part of my life learning numerology, reflexology, and sound color and vibration at the Esoteric Philosophy Center. I learned to take care of the mind and body as well as the soul. I was not so much religious then as I was spiritual.

On one of my visits to Houston before the move, I wrote "Tunnel Where the Beauty Hides," about the transition from a small town to a large city. The bustling freeways and bright city lights drew me much closer to the city.

Tunnel Where the Beauty Hides

I've pondered deep into my soul tonight, like drums beating vigorously, searching for that microscopic peace, not knowing it's lurking just beyond the door.

The ocean tides gush ever so quickly through my head, and the beat moves me forward, merging. In time I can't move fast enough. What rush comes over me as I peer into the tunnel.

Blue-red lights leap to catch my eyes. Sculptures of magnificent art speak harmoniously. Music sends me into a state of delusion. Serenity has found its home.

Faster than the hands of time, I surge. Visions of hope, love, and prosperity—they all stream before me like a mighty river. Clapping of acceptance sends me rushing forward.

Warmth fills my body as I pace on into infinity. The surge of the orchestra has totally filled me. Gliding to my depths now, I'm encased in the rhythms. Clouds from afar embrace my bosom.

I dare not once look back to regression. Searching my soul, I have touched backward in time. With that one touch I must not lose my search. Burdened with heavy feet to move forward. Standing still is not my destiny.

Struggle for survival is in my own hands. Behind lies deep purple petals of darkness. Minds are in a state of regression.

As I progress within my soul, I reach out and touch the outer rims of my peace.

Dealing with courts of monies, divorce, custody, etc., and job security, visions of hope, love, and prosperity appear as only a dim light at the end of the tunnel. The music still sends me merging with the expectancy of reaching those outer rims of my peace within the eminent future. Only legalities to slow time, and only for a moment.

My daughter and I made one last trip to Hamilton to close out the house. We rode a bus because our car had been repossessed just after the move to Houston. While riding the bus I recalled many memories and began to write this next piece.

Moving On. An Experience of Being

During the first part of my journey, my daughter and I rode a bus from Houston to Hamilton, and it felt as though we were running away. With each stripe of the highway we'd pass, at least a mile and many years of memories would go by.

We passed Marble Falls. Only while on a bus or being driven could I pay attention to these details. It is time. The painful process has begun. There was the first night we spent on our honeymoon. I recall the anticipation and slight anxiousness of it all. Even though I was pregnant, I was afraid and ashamed to undress in front of him. I hated my body, but he thought it beautiful.

Farther down the road I wrote this:

The hills of trees and grass aren't as green as they once were. A different time and space. Truly the autumn of my being. My soul feels so cold and empty inside.

I've counted these stacked soft clouds once before, but they seem more intense to me now. It's almost as if they are reaching out, embracing my bosom and comforting me through my pain. Before, they just hung, wishing to be admired for their beauty.

The entire heavens are more open today with my third eye than ever before. Letting go. What an experimental challenge. The universe has something to give me just as I have something to return. I've come to return the love and joy I have built and established around a small town and most of all, a small little ponderosa.

Gentle breezes of dust are visible on the ground—almost covering over the past lives we once had here.

I remember that roadside park where our little Sunday afternoon motorcycle family would come nestle under the trees and sip our beer. Even the weather blew very cold on our chests, sitting high rise on the seats. Only the engines to keep our inner thighs warm.

Yes. It is time. It is finished and over. It's all a memory. All but the work left to do ahead of me. The pain of truly letting it all . . . flow behind me.

It would be much easier to sleep through it all or remain out of my body. Especially since I have not slept for almost thirty hours. And since I'm not sure I can handle this journey of emotions alone. To accomplish this, though, I must remain well grounded.

These houses along the road must have lots of hidden feelings inside. They all remind me of mine. Rows of trees, vegetables, flowers, and rocks planted perfectly where no man can tread. I once had many spots where I knew exactly to the greatest degree on the ground where things were. I knew it was my private spot and no one could invade it. Many stones and flowers will be moved in the next couple of days after years of occupying. I guess the ground has been crying out to breathe for some time now. Well, now it will have its chance. The gentle snails as well as the scorpions are welcome to roam these areas, buried for so long.

I must remember the purple violet. I must indeed keep it in mind throughout this entire journey. It represents letting go. Perhaps I will just buy a purple violet candle before I hold my ritual and say my goodbyes. Inside I hold my mantras and oms and breaths of purple violet and soul aching to get free. It will be very spiritual healing and a time for new birth. *That's how my soul feels.*

Some of these rolling hills are just barren land. It's only in the distance that I can see new life. I too feel naked and exposed to whatever may be in store for me.

I have reached the old homestead now to say my goodbyes.

Wonderment.

I don't know a better word. It's still beautiful to me. It's almost empty now, and I feel our spirits brush by now and then as I gather and fold the curtains, discard the cracked papers, and unmount my unwanted shelves. There is intense love in the walls as I surface them with my hand.

The house was dark. The love exchanged was a new love. Love I once gave this house is now being given back to me. A warm *Thank you for taking care of me* is handed to me. My love . . . You've protected me from the cold and dangers of life. You've kept me feeling secure for many years. And now we must let each other go and lift some other soul through the same thing we once shared. The very energy around and inside you will always remain a part of me—just as I can see my energy dancing statically, then gracefully in the very pores of your wood.

There is the unfinished pond. It is a symbol of an unfinished love affair. Next lifetime, perhaps.

The garden is so full of weeds. Once we thought our garden was the finest in all these parts. It's only resting, you know. It is to be prepared for the next gardener.

The barn. It's full of memories and possessions from the earlier days of my marriage. It will be open tomorrow and readied to empty the next and final time I visit. To sell it, though, I had to come and take my final bow and let go. The grass, my grass, crunches under my feet. Have another drink and one from my heart. I give you back to the universe as I walk across your still blades here in this almost-full moon. It's only you and me. You'll be back next spring. You're only taking a rest for the next loving soul to take care of you again.

In three days, it will be a full moon: Libra, Aries, the unification of energies. It's almost full tonight, and what a lovely time to sit once again on the back steps and exchange energies with the tall hill behind all this.

The old swing sets and bicycle are rusting down. I remember my daughter with curly golden hair, swinging in the small set. It's much rustier than the taller gym set. Maybe we'll take it along with us.

That little girl is growing into a beautiful young woman.

Yes, it's time. We have taken far too much of each other's energy and held it for ransom. You've suffered being painted, mowed, watered, lived in and on, and loved much too long. I've suffered being nonexistent by my non-activity. Not letting go kept all my energy tied up here where I no longer belong. Nature will care for you until you are bought, I promise you. Just as this cool night breeze sweeps my face and across these pages, so will it sweep your rooftops with God-sent love.

That cute little daughter of mine came running up to me today and said, "I found some things I can use: a penny, a hanger, some nails, and a paintbrush." She too has some memories. I am not the only one having to say goodbye to the past.

The flowers are all dug and transplanted to where care and love will be plentiful.

The curtain is closing, and I give my final bow.

I want to *fight* and to *throw* bodies out into the universe. Leaving the old home is incredibly hard.

But—I give you back to the universe. Give me strength and will in turn. I hardly ask anything in return.

But I'm asking of you because of your dynamic energy exchange. My love, until the next life.

Once again, I returned to my home in Houston. Troubled, I made a trip to Galveston and wrote another piece.

To Till the Soul

Oh . . . great waters of darkness. Embrace me with your soul so we become one, for I am troubled, empty, and without.

Please send me answers as the whitecaps of your knees fold gently toward me.

You have carried me on your shoulders for hours now, and still there are no answers for this troubled soul. Embrace me tight as I search for the peaceful meaning of the rocking lullaby you continue to chant.

Stop and imagine yourself without shoulders. Who would carry us to our destiny? No sand between my toes? A beach without sand is an hourglass without time. Yet what is time? An ocean without waves angers and tempts the forces as does my body without essence of being.

Each is akin to the other, and all needs are equal parts to harvest rows of production not yet in sight.

Let me ask you, old dark body of water: Have you ever felt alone? Have you hungered for calm and serenity? Ever felt as though you would explode? Please, still your waters long enough for my spent mind to grasp your givings.

The waters that God created spoke, saying this to me:

"Troubled soul, you asked me if I ever felt alone. Well, yes, when raging storms kept all of you away, I was left out here alone. You ask if I hunger for calm and serenity. These feelings are the afterbirth of the storms and are fulfilled once again when visitors come back.

"I speak to you, lost soul, for that is what you are. Go, child, on bent knees, looking toward the heavens, as my whitecaps fold gently toward you, uplifting you gently. In search of mighty answers from powerful forces, you have begun to till the soul."

The home in Houston was quite different from the farmhouse. The courtyard was always buzzing at my Houston home and certainly back in my drinking days. You could see my neighbor and me sitting on a roof with a cooler of beer or doing something like cutting tree limbs in a thunderstorm. Neither of those things were approved of in the townhome complex where I lived. My drinking days finally took a toll on me. Many dark days passed until I decided on a sober date of September 9, 1999—a "one" day in numerology, which means new beginnings. I had changed everything about myself since my move from Hamilton.

We had many Christmas parties in that house in Houston. Amey was the cocktail waitress, and I would put on my act. Or we would have a professional piano player friend come and play as we all sang. Fabulous times.

I always kept my flower garden and patio immaculate. Neighbors would bring their children to take pictures of my hydrangeas, which were a carpet of purple hues.

Now after forty-two years it is time to make another colossal move, this time to a town near Dallas called Forney.

With many hard stairs in my home to climb and having gotten a diagnosis of severe osteoporosis, I think it's time to move in with my daughter so she can take care of me as I get older. I have added a bedroom to her house, and we added a covered patio, fully screened in for my sweet little Sadie Lady cat.

How do I say goodbye to friends and business contacts I've known for so many years? How do I part with a place I have called home for forty-two years? There is a great tug on my heartstrings to relocate my being once more.

I made a quick trip to Forney to transplant my flowers. The journey has truly begun. Scattered brain matters have me running in five different directions. But now it's time to settle my being in a new home with my daughter.

Now with a crystal in my pocket for clarity and an orange candle burning for courage, I must say goodbye to my friends. No more swimming parties or lunches out or visiting neighbors on the benches. We've danced and sung until the last party was over.

Time to attend to the business of packing and saying goodbye to the homestead. Our move date is April 28,

2023, which is a "three" day in numerology. It represents great social spirit and success in all I will undertake.

It colors my heart with joy as I weave the threads of my journey. It is just that the struggle of letting go is so real. It's just a state of mind that I have been given control of. I have been down this rigid and muddy road before. Profuse teardrops hit these pages as I put one foot before the other. With soppy wet feet I will carry on and ready myself for the next move in my life. Varied emotions have come and gone like a mighty whirlwind.

Once again it is time. Tonight, I had a going-away party. Forty-some people came to Los Tios Mexican Restaurant, a local favorite, to bid me farewell. Tales of old were hilarious, tears were shed, and people brought lots of cards and gifts. A wonderful time was had by all. In another four weeks it will be time for the big move.

This party awakened poignant memories of good times.

It will be full circle, moving back to a semi-country setting. Riding our John Deere tractor is truly a hoot for me. We have eight large, raised vegetable gardens, which have been planted. We have acreage enough to have redbuds and mimosas and whatever we want to plant. It is extremely peaceful.

I am leaving Houston to go to a beautiful white dream. The bridge to cross is not as devastating as the last move, for I will be back with my daughter. I will have my mini she shed in the corner of the three-car garage. I have two pieces of Italian marble that were shipped and sent by train to one of my old job sites, Bayou Bend Apartment Towers. The man I worked for gave them to me, and they will be tops for my workbench. I am looking forward to so many things.

Upon my visits to Forney I saw brilliant sunrises on the back patio of my new home. It is so peaceful and still. No gunshots or sirens nearby to listen to. Just the many redbirds at the feeders and songbirds in a tree with their beautiful songs. I have taken walks down the road to meet new neighbors.

I've been to the nearby lake and waterfall to meditate. The rustling of the leaves brings on the new spring with trees budding out and ducks playing in the waters. It's another safe place for me just as the park near my home in Houston was. There I did a lot of writing, meditating, and praying while enjoying the music and watching people feed ducks and geese.

Just like that I will morph into a new way of life in Forney, Texas. And once again, serenity will find its home for me.

ABOUT THE AUTHOR

RIKKI (CINDY) SHAW

Named Cindy at birth, Rikki Shaw reinvented herself for the stage at age thirty. An accomplished ventriloquist and drummer, she has performed for audiences all over Texas. Offstage, she is a mom, grandma, and former nurse. In the last forty years, she has come full circle from small town to big city and back again, leaving her painful past behind with her old name. As you delve into Rikki's esoteric and eccentric viewpoints, you will learn how to navigate the process of letting go and embracing new identities.

Chapter 13

GIVE GLORY AND PRAISE

Debi Choi

"We can't control what happens, but we can choose how we respond."

Right as I was neck-deep into a pantry reorganization, the phone rang.

"Is this Mrs. Choi?" the caller asked. "This is Susie from the Prisma Health Trauma Center. We have your husband here."

Then she handed the phone to my husband.

"Honey, I'm not walking away from this one."

I could not possibly have prepared myself for what I saw when I walked into that trauma room, or for the total disruption and radical change that was about to consume our lives. Not for just that day or two weeks or two months, but forever.

I arrived at the hospital but didn't even realize I had parked in the wrong parking area and entered the wrong wing. As I walked through the building trying to find my husband, I was in full panic mode, but I kept saying to myself, *Don't make assumptions, don't make any conclusions without the facts.* The logical and analytical side of my brain kept my emotions in check.

I was in a nightmare. Lost. There was a storm blowing around me. The wind was blowing me from side to side and from person to person. No one would help me. *Can't they see me, hear me? I am but a ghost, where I can't be seen or heard. Can they not see there is a crisis and I need help? Why won't anyone help me?*

I was lost in the hospital and couldn't find the trauma area where my husband was. Everyone kept telling me I couldn't get to him from the wing I was in. I kept stopping people in uniform and asking them to please take me to him. They kept taking me to someone else who tried to help me, but each person said, "He isn't in our system," or "I am not able to take you there from here."

Finally, someone heard me. Someone saw the urgency, the panic. She directed me to a chair and said, "I will have someone come get you and take you to him."

Time has stopped. . . . Time is endless. . . . The wait is endless. . . . Each second feels like an hour, and no one comes.

I looked up and saw my husband's daughter walking toward me. I had called her on my way to the hospital. She grabbed me and held me and said, "Come on, Momma, I'm going to take you to Pops. But I've seen him and it's bad, so brace yourself."

I stepped into the trauma room and lay eyes on Will, the love of my life. He tried to smile at me through a drug-induced state, assuring me he was alive. *Yes, he is alive. Whatever else happens, whatever else we have to face, he is ALIVE!*

Oh my goodness, there is so much blood—dripping, still bleeding, dripping onto the floor.

My husband was on his way to work on a beautiful sunny Sunday when a car drove straight into the side of his motor-cycle and hit his left side, sending him flying into the air.

The trauma doctor began to explain to me some of Will's injuries. He had a gash down his left arm, but fortunately, the trauma team had cleared his neck and spine of any damage. Their primary concern was the left foot. I listened carefully and understood that they were waiting on ortho-pedic and surgical consults to further assess the damage. I asked to see what we were dealing with. The more hesitant the doctor was to show me the wounded area, the more anxious I became. "It's bad," she said, "and I don't think you should see it."

"I need to see it," I said. Again, my logical and analytical brain kicked aside my emotions. I knew I had to see what we were dealing with so I could know how to move forward. When I told the doctor that, nurses surrounded me in case I needed support.

When the yellow drape was lifted, I saw macerated flesh stripped away from the bone and half of Will's foot hanging by a small amount of flesh. The upper half of the foot was attached, but it was so severely damaged that I knew we were looking at intensive surgeries and a long recovery. I still didn't know what lay ahead, though. You know that game you play as a child? *If I don't say it, it isn't true. If I don't think it, it won't happen.* I was playing that game in my head. *Yes, the damage is bad, but medicine has come so far, they will fix this. Yes, there is a long road ahead, but we will get through this. He is alive and we will get through this*!

Maybe it was best I didn't know what was ahead yet. Could I have handled it in that moment?

The next update we got was chilling. The toes had lost all blood flow, and the damage was so severe that the toes would need to be amputated. We were taking baby bites as they were fed to us, and again I thought, *It's not great news, but it's not so bad. It's just the toes, not the foot.*

As they wheeled him toward the operating room for surgery, we stopped in the hall outside the doors, and my husband asked me to pray with him. The attending surgeon bowed his head as I prayed for strength for everyone who was so kind and caring and making decisions for him. I asked God to give them wisdom and knowledge. And to give us peace throughout the waiting period.

Will and I had discussed the damage before he went into surgery, so I knew our expectations were that they would save as much of the foot as possible and planned to remove only the toes. The surgeons had already vaguely discussed possible walking challenges and that he might want to consider an above-the-ankle amputation. My husband was clear, though: *Just the toes. Save as much of the foot as you can.*

As the afternoon turned into evening and evening turned into night, we paced the empty surgical waiting area. It was late when an attending surgeon came out to update us. The toes could not be saved. They were going to have to amputate more than they initially anticipated because of the maceration and damage. Again, the option of an above-the-ankle amputation was discussed, and I kept strong in my husband's wishes to save all they could. We could go back and do a revision, but we couldn't undo an aggressive amputation.

It was now after midnight, and my stepdaughter and I were anxiously waiting for him to be in recovery so we could see him. And finally, the surgeon came out to say it was over, that Will was in recovery. He would need more surgery in the next few days so doctors could continue to clean the damaged area, and they would assess how the amputation was healing. At each surgery they would determine if further amputation revision was required.

Oh, how I wanted to sob. I wanted to crawl up in the corner and cry about what was ahead for my strong warrior, whose feet had carried him so many miles, being strong for me and our family, working day after day to support our needs. He is such a strong Samoan man by birth and a warrior by heart, and I had never seen him down, sick, without strength.

I was so glad that he took his first look at his wrapped foot while he was still recovering from anesthesia. When I saw the stub, I was shocked, and gut-wrenching sorrow engulfed me. I knew the shock was going to be awful for him. It wasn't until the next day that he realized how much they had taken and that our life was now forever changed.

Early the following morning, I had a call from the state trooper who had been at the scene. He said there was a bond hearing for the driver of the vehicle, and that we had a right to be there and speak to the judge. He said a state victim advocate would be calling to confirm the place and time and would meet us at the courthouse.

Before he called, we knew very little about the driver who had hit Will. In his shock, my husband thought it was a man. But it was a woman in her mid-thirties who was high on drugs. She had nodded off at the wheel, and as she fell asleep, her foot hit the gas pedal and she accelerated and ran straight into him. The impact slowed her down and stopped her in a ditch. Will had saved her life, in a sense, by taking the blow instead of her driving headfirst into the ditch at full speed.

We had never really thought about being a "victim." That word had never been part of our vocabulary, so it was foreign to us to use in relation to him. But as I spoke to various people such as the trooper, the state victim advocate, and the victim advocate from Mothers Against Drunk Driving (MADD), we realized that was exactly what our family was: the victim of someone who had made a very poor choice.

I showed up at the courthouse at the hearing time, but they had technical issues, so we were left sitting for three hours, waiting for the judge to be ready to see us. They were bringing the driver in through a virtual call, and they had to wait for it to work so she could be present.

As I sat there with the victim advocates and my daughter, I didn't know what I was going to say. I had no words. I had not slept in almost forty-eight hours. I was in shock. Speechless! What do you say?

Finally we were led into the tiny little courtroom and I saw face-to-face the person who had brought this dramatic change to our lives.

You just aren't prepared for this type of event, and I don't know what I should have felt, but all I could express to the judge was gratitude. Our family was so grateful that my husband and our Poppy was coming home to us. But the next person might not be so fortunate. My desire was that the judge would not allow others to be put in danger. Our hope was that this incident would change the driver in a positive way so that she could turn her life around.

I told the judge that my mantra since I had found out Will was injured was this: In spite of this, I will give God glory and praise. That has been what our family has focused on since this happened. Glory and praise and thanks to God!

The driver sobbed as I spoke, shaking her head and saying, "Oh my God, I didn't know," over and over. Because she had passed out from the drugs and was not coherent at the scene, she had no idea she had caused any damage or great bodily injury to anyone until that moment at the bail hearing.

Although we were told by the South Carolina Highway Patrol, the state victim advocate, and the MADD advocate that there was *no way* bail would be denied, because it typically isn't, even when the case involves loss of life, the judge immediately denied bond.

We all gasped. *Praise God for the lives that will be saved by this decision*!

The judge said she had never seen a victim's family give gratitude and not ask for justice.

As we walked out of the courtroom, I was trembling uncontrollably, adrenaline rushing through my body. The MADD advocate said she had never heard or seen anything like it.

I can tell you it was not my words I spoke that day, but words God had placed in my heart to be able to speak with love and forgiveness and gratitude.

I wondered where those "normal" emotions—shock, anger, the desire for justice—were during that time. They were hiding, waiting to surprise me down the road when I least expected it. Sneaking up on me at unexpected moments.

A month later the driver had her second bond hearing, and we were asked if we wanted to write a victim's statement.

My husband asked me to draft it, and then he would approve it. We asked the court's victim advocate to read it on our behalf.

It was surreal that day, watching the orange jumpsuits be led into the courtroom with chains on their hands and feet. Like sitting on the sidelines, watching a TV show, or like it was happening to someone else. As each prisoner filed in, I scanned them for her face. I wanted her to look at us, acknowledge our presence, our pain. As she came in and took a seat, she never even looked our way, as if she had already healed and moved past the atrocity she had caused.

Her grandmother spoke on her behalf, saying she was a good mother, had a job waiting for her, and that her babies needed her. As she returned to her seat, she looked our way and said, "I'm so sorry. I'm so very sorry."

There it was. There was that anger inside of me! How dare someone talk about her having a job waiting for her. Why should she be able to go back to work when my husband was permanently disabled? Of course her children needed her. So did our family need our husband, grandfather, and father. The whole person he was. She could get all that back and be fully restored, but it would never be that way for our family again.

And then the advocate read our letter to the judge. There was chatter throughout the courtroom as lawyers discussed their upcoming cases. But as she began to read, a hush fell on the room, and everyone began to listen and hear. No chatter, just a quiet stillness.

I had tried to capture the thoughts and feelings my husband had shared. I've shared the statement here.

Victim Statement—Choi

When I was told I could make a victim statement, I was at a loss for words. I wanted to take the easy way out and say nothing, trusting that the court would see the trauma Ms. McGill has caused and the danger to society that she is.

Since the incident I have gone through 4 surgeries. As soon as I was transported to the ER, an emergency amputation had to be performed of the foot. The first two surgeries, my amputation was left open, and the open area had to be scrubbed with a wire brush to remove debris and possible contamination. I cannot express how painful that was despite anesthesia and multiple pain medications. On the 3rd surgery the amputation was finally closed. The surgeons were hopeful that the flap they created to cover the amputation would heal properly. I lived for 8 weeks, not knowing if further revision would be necessary and if I would lose the rest of my foot all the way above the ankle. We are still too early in the process to know the full extent of the damage; however, we have lived with it long enough to realize how dramatically it has changed and impacted my life and the life of my family.

I must learn to walk all over again, and I don't know how long that will even take so I can go back to work and be a support for my family.

I was always very physical, being a runner and weightlifting, but now taking stairs [is] difficult.

I live with ghost pains and for the rest of my life I will be on medication because my brain doesn't know that I am missing my foot and the nerve endings are always sensitive and tingling to the point of painful.

I would like this to change Ms. McGill to be a better person. Clearly, she has some lessons to learn.

My hope is that in the learning process she is not allowed to be free to cause more damage to someone else or loss of life or limb to the next person. If you see fit to grant bond, my request is that at the very least, a GPS monitoring ankle bracelet is attached, license [is] revoked, and counseling is provided to Ms. McGill.

I hope that my loss is a good enough price for her to learn her lesson and can save the life of the next person by not endangering innocent people around her.

I have always taught my children, Do Good, Be Good, and Never Give Up. This is what I wish for Ms. McGill to learn.

Ms. McGill was given a large bond with house arrest, ankle monitoring, and routine drug testing.

For six months, I couldn't leave my husband's side and sat right next to him wherever he was. If he was in bed, I was sitting next to him working. If he woke up and I wasn't there, he would call for me, and I would rush up the stairs and let him know I was on my way. Sometimes I would just be in the next room. Life came to a full halt for both of us.

It's been months now. We are still walking this journey and don't yet know its purpose or where the road will lead. As humans do, we planned. He would be back to work in six months, and then it was eight months later, and then nine and then ten. We don't know when he will be back to work or if he can even return to his former profession as a truck driver. The damage was so severe that ten months later, we are just now seeing him well enough to be fit for a pros-thetic, and then he must learn to walk again.

The man who had almost reached his million-mile safe driv-er's award has not driven in almost a year.

The runner must learn to run again.

Some days we feel fear, worry, and anxiety about provision, the future. We don't know what the future looks like.

Until something like this happens, you don't know the value of being able to do simple activities like bathing, getting up and down stairs, washing your hair, and getting in and out of a vehicle. You don't have to be afraid of falling, or wonder, *Will this facility do a good job of accommodating people with disabilities?*

During this time, we have found laughter. We have found humor.

He has named his foot Stubby.

And people have sent us jokes like, "I heard Will went for a job interview. But he couldn't get a foot in the door."

Will likes to prank us by acting like he is waking up from a nightmare in which he lost a foot. Then he looks at his foot and says, "Oh my God, it wasn't a nightmare, it really happened." And as we stand there in horror, trying to figure out how to respond and support him, he breaks into huge laughter.

It has been a joint, family effort. If one of us had not chosen joy and gratitude and chosen to walk a different emotional path or journey, then we would have each felt alone. But together we are strong. On the days one person stumbles, the other one reaches out a hand and says, "I'm here. We will do this together."

We can't control what has happened, but we can choose how we respond. And we choose gratitude and joy for life!

ABOUT THE AUTHOR

DEBI
CHOI

Debi Choi is a long-time owner of an accounting firm who geeks out on numbers and excel spreadsheets. After founding a Facebook group serving 6500 industry professionals and supporting hundreds of entrepreneurs in their business growth, she was looking forward to retirement planning while also working to adopt her two grandchildren. Then, an intoxicated driver changed her family's life and her plans. She shares her story with transparency, deep insight and humor in the hope of helping others face trauma with grace and gratitude. Debi and her husband are now working on founding a nonprofit to support victims of intoxicated driving accidents. To connect with Debi you can follow her on Facebook @debi.choi or email her at debichoi@sagegrowthadvisors.com

AFTERWORD

The publication of this book, *Shine Your Light*, brings to a close an incredible collaborative book journey. This book is the last of a 3-book series in which thirty-four women have come forward to boldly write their stories and publish them in a book for all the world to read.

When I first joined forces with our publisher and co-creator of the LIGHTbeamers She Gets Published program, Lanette Pottle — we only had one book in mind. After we started writing with the fourteen women who came forward for our first book, *Elevate Your Voice*, we soon had a waiting list of other women raising their hands for future book writing opportunities.

Almost seamlessly, the titles and visions for each of the books came together, and Lanette and I knew we had three books that needed to be written:

Elevate Your Voice
Step Into Your Brave
Shine Your Light

We were intentional about the book titles being in that order because when you examine what it takes for one to share their story so publicly, you see that it starts with making a decision to use your voice — deciding that you have something to say. Claiming it. Owning it. Elevating your voice is the first step.

Then, you have to take action. Stepping into your brave is doing the thing despite being a little nervous or unsure. Taking daily action towards excavating your story, and sitting down to write and make edits requires you to step into your brave because you don't always feel like you know what you are doing.

The authors who've written their stories for our collaborative book series have all had moments of great uncertainty — questioning if they were gettng the story right, feeling at times like the story wasn't good enough, and fretting repeatedly that once the story was released publicly nobody would want to read it. Yet, they took action and did it anyway.

"Step into your Brave" is a motto we've carried throughout this writing process.

And finally, we get to *Shine Your Light*. The final piece of writing and publishing a book is the act of releasing our words out into the world. I've had the great pleasure of working in the world of storytelling for more than thirty years in my career — and I can honestly say there is something really special that happens when you share your story so that others can receive it. You shine the light. Our stories are the light we get to shine for other people — to serve as a reminder or an encouragement they might need as they travel their own journey.

It feels really, really good to know that your story can actually be used to do some good in this world.

Ultimately, that is our hope with the release of this third collaborative book with the thirteen women's stories you've just read — we hope that our stories will connect you back to something in your own story, that you will discover something you need in order to continue on your path, and that you will be inspired in some way to take positive action in your life. May the light shine for you in a way that feels warm and illuminating.

xo,
April

READ ALL THREE!

www.lightbeamers.com/books

ACKNOWLEDGEMENTS

Writing this book and others in this series took a great many people behind the scenes — most of whom never get the credit, see their name on the back cover, or get invited to do podcast interviews during a book launch. Yet we couldn't do it without them.

A few we'd like to purposely call by name: Dyan Escolano, Christine Roxas, and Felice Perez — the amazing team members at LIGHTbeamers who pour their hearts into our projects and help us shine in countless ways. Your dedication to our mission at LIGHTbeamers is felt. Thank you for bringing your heart into everything we do, even from halfway around the world!

To our editor, Laurel Robinson. Thank you for putting so much of your time and talent into our words. Words are powerful, and you've helped us make the most of ours. Your thoughtful notes and suggestions have pushed us to be better writers, and it's been a joy to have you work on this project.

To our book designer and formatter, Ashley Hinson Dhakal. Since day one, you've been able to take our ideas and truly bring them to life on the front and back covers, and on the pages in between. Thank you!

A special thanks to fellow author and prolific writer, Emma G. Rose, for stepping in to teach our authors about the art of crafting a killer bio. Her approach really helped us take a much more fun and creative approach to writing something that can often feel extremely hard! Thank you! Thank you!!

And to our publisher and co-leader of the Lightbeamers She Gets Published Author Program, Lanette Pottle. Your guidance has been invaluable. Taking a group of women through the process of becoming first-time published authors requires a firm grip and a gentle touch — and you possess both. It's an honor to walk these books to the finish line with you!

Finally, a personal note to my family and the families of all my co-authors. Thank you for the time you've given us to squirrel away at our writing desks, or the time we've spent on social media preparing our audiences for this book. Thank you for your supportive words of encouragement when we needed it. And mostly, thank you for believing our stories matter.

WORK WITH APRIL

April Adams Pertuis helps mission-driven female entrepreneurs and business leaders use their stories to amplify their impact and income by increasing their visibility on stages, in books, and in digital media.

April's expertise spans more than thirty years in the storytelling and media industry, and her work has appeared on CBS, HGTV, the Food Network, the Huffington Post, and Fox.

Beyond all her career achievements, April is best known for her positive outlook on life, magnetic energy, and cheerleader-type of support. When you get around April, you start to believe anything is possible. She operates from a standpoint of "no woman left behind," and it's what has helped her build a wildly engaged online global community reaching thousands of women in more than ten countries.

April has personally worked with hundreds of women to build their brand authority through podcast appearances, speaking engagements, and book launches. She has a philosophy that "everybody has a story . . . and when you share your story, you shine a light."

A former television journalist and producer turned storytelling and visibility expert, April is the CEO and founder of LIGHTbeamers, a training and coaching company helping women leaders harness the power of their stories. She is the author of two Amazon international bestselling books, and is a highly sought-after speaker and women's empowerment thought leader.

Through her work at LIGHTbeamers, April facilitates group coaching programs, an online visibility training membership, and offers direct one-to-one support to clients. If you'd like to explore going deeper with your story and using it as the powerful engine it is, connect with April to explore what your story can do for you at www.lightbeamers.com/apply

ABOUT LIGHTBEAMERS

April Adams Pertuis' passion for storytelling and creating community with women led her to create LIGHTbeamers – a safe space to explore your story, find support, and get training on how to excavate the layers of your story to use in a positive, powerful way.

Using the weekly story prompts and private community, members have open and honest conversations about life, business, personal growth, and spirituality. It's a place to learn more about storytelling as it relates to your own life and business.

LIGHTbeamers also offers online courses, group coaching, and training programs, as well as high-level mentorship for women leaders who are ready to step into their brave and share their story with more people.

Members are CEOs, entrepreneurs, spiritual and civic leaders, change-makers, missionaries, teachers, and healers. They use their story every day to create community, affect change, and make a positive impact in the world by shining their light.

To learn more about the LIGHTbeamers community and suite of programs, go to www.lightbeamers.com

ABOUT THE INSIDE STORY PODCAST

The Inside Story Podcast takes you behind the curtain of the biggest success stories of entrepreneurs, thought leaders, and change-makers . . . people who have walked through fire and come out on the other side brighter. They aren't mechanical or scripted. They are unabashedly authentic and real. And they are generating massive success & fulfillment as a result!

The goal of the Inside Story is to inspire you to think about your own story, and learn to share it so it can shine a light for others.

Listen in to discover unique storytelling tips and mechanics that will empower you to tell your story in a whole new way.

Learn more and listen at www.lightbeamers.com/podcast

ABOUT POSITIVITY LADY PRESS

Positivity Lady Press is a small indie publishing imprint dedicated to awakening possibilities in the lives of women through inspirational, self help and personal development books. The press is owned and operated by Lanette Pottle.

WE BELIEVE when we encourage, empower, and elevate women, the world becomes a kinder, more compassionate place.

WE BELIEVE when women rise to their full potential it generates an endless supply of creative solutions to the challenges facing our world.

WE BELIEVE thoughtful collaboration among women accelerates the speed and the reach of positive impact we can make.

WE BELIEVE women's voices matter and a book is a powerful way to amplify them.

If you have ideas for collaborative projects elevating the voices of women, connect with Lanette directly through email at lanette@lanettepottle.com

ABOUT OUR PAY-IT-FORWARD PARTNERSHIP

 **100% of royalties from Amazon sales of this book will be directed to KIVA, with a special interest** given to funding micro-loans to help women around the globe to start and grow businesses.

Kiva is an international nonprofit, founded in 2005 in San Francisco, with a mission to expand financial access to help underserved communities thrive.

They do this by crowdfunding loans and unlocking capital for the underserved, improving the quality and cost of financial services, and addressing the underlying barriers to financial access around the world. Through Kiva's work, students can pay for tuition, women can start businesses, farmers are able to invest in equipment and families can afford needed emergency care.

Learn more at www.kiva.org